Claiming Your Victories

A Concise Guide to College Success

Linda Stevens Hjorth

DeVry Institute of Technology–DuPage Campus, Illinois

Houghton Mifflin Company   Boston   New York

Director of Student Success Programs: Barbara A. Heinssen
Associate Editors: Melissa Plumb and Douglas W. Texter
Associate Project Editor: Patricia English
Editorial Assistant: Lauren M. Gagliardi
Senior Production/Design Coordinator: Sarah Ambrose
Senior Manufacturing Coordinator: Sally Culler

Cover Design: Minko T. Dimov, MinkoImages
Illustrations: Nick Jateano

Printed in the U.S.A.
Library of Congress Catalog Card Number: 99-71964

ISBN: 0-395-72735-9

123456789–PO–03 02 01 00 99

*This book is dedicated to every student who has the desire to learn
and to every teacher who is willing to create
challenging teaching paradigms that will help students learn. This book
is also dedicated to my daughter Robyn, a high school graduate of the
class of 2000, who as a college freshman, along with all other
college freshmen reading this book, will be leaving one
threshold in life and crossing another.*

Contents

Chapter 2 Critical Thinking and Problem Solving 21

Chapter 3 Setting Goals and Managing Time 35

Chapter **4**

Study Strategies 57

Chapter **5**

Note-Taking 83

Chapter **6**

Test-Taking 103

Chapter 7

Writing   123

Chapter **8**

Relationships   139

Preface

Claiming Your Victories: A Concise Guide to College Success will help to mentor students along their step-by-step journey through the world of higher education. I have chosen a workbook format to give students easy access to strategies that support success in college. *Claiming Your Victories* provides easy-to-read suggestions that will encourage motivation, guide goal setting, augment critical thinking abilities, and enhance time management strategies. The text provides students with ways in which to polish the note-taking, test-taking, and writing techniques that they currently possess. But strategies and techniques are not the only necessary components of student success. Perseverance and the ability to take personal responsibility for decisions made in daily life form the needed complements to academic skills. *Claiming Your Victories* will help students to develop these qualities.

The material in this text has been chosen to provide guidance and support as students strive to meet their academic and personal goals. Suggestions are provided within a concise format so that students can quickly read, practice, and assimilate the skills that are essential for college success.

It is my goal to involve students in the active learning process in ways that promote improved study skills, self-examination, responsible decision making, and integration into the college community. The following features have been created to reinforce these goals:

▶ **Checklists** Designed to assess knowledge and skills relating to text content, a checklist starts each chapter. It is a fun and quick self-report that targets weaknesses and strengths. By assessing their own strengths before they read the chapter, students can easily identify subject areas on which they may need to concentrate. The checklists also provide a concise preview of each chapter.

▶ **Exercises** Exercises provide students with an opportunity to practice or analyze strategies about which they have read. It is one thing to read about study strategies; it is quite another to practice and implement them. Each exercise integrates a variety of learning styles.

▶ **Quick Checks** The margin contains boxes with questions that check students' understanding of chapter information. Students answer the questions to increase their comprehension of presented information as they progress through each chapter.

▶ **Step Inside** This feature highlights the student support systems available on college campuses. By increasing their awareness of resources, students will feel more "at home" in the college community.

▶ **Role Plays** Each chapter contains one open-ended role play that allows students to articulate perceptions about themselves, others, and the world around them. Because students create the ending to each role play, they are encouraged to speak from the characters' perspectives while developing their own voices. Role plays reinforce teamwork as students interact in groups to create and act out scenarios.

▶ **Reviews** Each chapter ends with a review section. Each review item is numbered to correspond to one of the original objectives; this correspondence provides a way to check learning. Students can review the chapters by reading the objectives and writing down everything they know about each one. Then they can compare the list to the review at the end of each chapter. If there are specific topics on which they need to concentrate more, students can go back and review them within the chapter.

▶ **Student Quotations**   Quotations representative of student attitudes at colleges across North America offer learners a fresh student perspective on the subject being studied.

▶ **Visuals**   Graphs, diagrams, flowcharts, cartoons, and photographs throughout the text increase learning, provide reviews, and supplement lectures and classroom activities.

▶ **Definitions**   Listed in the margins of the text, definitions provide a quick reference for understanding. These words are redefined in the glossary at the back of the text.

▶ **Internet Exercises**   Each chapter contains an Internet exercise that correlates with the chapter's content. By completing these exercises, students can become familiar with the Internet as a resource while learning more information about specific student success strategies.

The Instructor's Resource Manual

The Instructor's Resource Manual supports the information provided in the text by offering suggestions for course planning, exercises, lectures, syllabi, and videos that will encourage motivation, guide goal setting, augment critical thinking strategies, and enhance time management strategies. This manual offers teaching techniques that will encourage students to polish their note-taking, test-taking, and writing skills while presenting exercises that encourage self-understanding and intrinsic motivation.

Videos to Supplement Lectures

Roundtable Discussion videotapes were created by Houghton Mifflin Company to support student success courses. *Study Strategies* covers the four primary proficiencies (note-taking, reading, memory, and test-taking) and introduces specific techniques to enhance the learning process for each set of skills. *Life Skills* examines three areas that support student success (goal setting, time management, and stress management).

For information on ordering the Roundtable Discussion videotapes, please contact your Houghton Mifflin Company representative, or telephone the Faculty Service Center at 1-800-733-1717.

Acknowledgments

No project can be completed without the support of others. Thanks to the following: all the students from my classes who have taught me the essence of student success; students whose quotations are included in *Claiming Your Victories;* DeVry Institute of Technology, DuPage Campus students and their professors—Bill Hayes, Eilene McBride, Beth McFarland, Christine Lewinski, Shawn Schumacher, and Dean Sandra Graham—who class-tested *Claiming Your Victories* and provided pertinent feedback and analysis; Gary Hoskins, a student at Aurora University, Aurora, IL, for creating the cartoons; Pam Turburan and Lisa Butler for their creative and insightful support; and Maria Bakalis, professor at Waubonsee College, for developing the role plays.

Thanks are also due to all of the reviewers for their direction and suggestions:

Diane Adams, *Reading Area Community College*, PA

John D. Barton, *Utah State University—Uintah Basin Branch Campus*

Maureen Brower, *State University of New York, Stonybrook*, NY

Sharon Cordell, *Roane State Community College*, TN

L. Ray Drinkwater, *John Tyler Community College*, VA

Peter J. Quinn, *Commonwealth College—Richmond Campus*, VA

Tom Rossi, *Broome Community College*, NY

Shawn A. Schumacher, *DeVry Institute of Technology—DuPage Campus*, IL

Jacqueline Simon, *Rider University*, NJ

Manning L. Smith, *Garrett Community College*, MD

John A. Turnbull, *Connors State College*, OH

Peggy Weissinger, *Indiana University—Purdue University at Indianapolis*

At Houghton Mifflin I received support and help from Alison Zetterquist, Vice President of New Ventures; Barbara Heinssen, Director of Student Success Programs; Bill Webber, former Director of Student Success Programs; Melissa Plumb, former Associate Editor; Douglas W. Texter, Associate Editor; Shani Fisher, Editorial Assistant, Patricia English, Associate Project Editor; and Lauren M. Gagliardi, Editorial Assistant.

Finally, special thanks must go to my family: my husband, Craig, and our children, Josh, Robyn, and Kelly, all of whom endured my late nights and early mornings of writing and were willing to wait until the next sentence was finished before asking questions. Special thanks also go to Irv and Irma Overmyer, who taught me from a very early age that attaining an education is one of life's most important achievements.

To Students

As a professor who has taught Student Success Strategies courses for fifteen years, I welcome you to college. The adventures that you will experience in the next few years will provide you with the foundation for a new career and a new life. Adjusting to the college environment is a challenge. Each day that you learn something new, meet someone different, create goals for success, and overcome challenges, you are experiencing college victories. I want *Claiming Your Victories: A Concise Guide to College Success* to support your endeavor to be successful. If you have questions or feedback regarding this text, please take time to write me a note (via the Director, Student Success Programs, Houghton Mifflin Company, 215 Park Avenue South, New York, NY 10003). I look forward to hearing from you.

Best wishes to you as you start your new collegiate experiences.

Linda Stevens Hjorth

CHAPTER 1

Victories in College

OBJECTIVES

By the end of this chapter, you will be able to . . .

1. **Comprehend that each positive college experience is a personal victory.**

2. **Understand more clearly why you are attending college.**

3. **Understand your personal learning style and integrate it into your study habits and your career.**

4. **Understand how brain dominance relates to study strategies.**

5. **Take charge of your education.**

6. **Understand how intrinsic and extrinsic motivators correlate to college success.**

7. **Identify campus resources and learn how to use them.**

I CAME TO COLLEGE BECAUSE . . . CHECKLIST

You may find yourself in the middle of tests or studying late at night and wonder: Why am I doing this? This checklist will help clarify your motivation for attending college and will serve as a gentle reminder to stay motivated.

Place a check mark next to reasons with which you identify. Star your top two reasons. Be sure to add any that are not listed.

I came to college because . . .

_____ I enjoy reading, learning, and being in school.

_____ Mom and dad encouraged me.

_____ I want to learn skills that will enhance my future career.

_____ I am smart, and college is where I belong.

_____ I know that the only way I can make money is to have a college degree.

_____ My girlfriend (boyfriend) came to this school, and I do not want to be far away from her (him).

_____ I think that college is the best place to prove to everyone in the family how successful I can really be.

_____ I want to become more knowledgeable.

_____ As a middle manager, I was laid off. The only way for me to make it financially is to go back to school.

_____ I am a mother with two children. They are in school now, and I can finally go to school to achieve my dream of a higher education.

_____ I know that through college I can increase my athletic skills.

_____ I know that through college I can increase my academic skills.

_____ College will provide me with the opportunity to meet new people.

_____ I am a single parent and must learn new skills in order to support my family.

_____ Graduation means a great deal to me. I want to walk across the stage with my head high, feeling proud.

Fill in other reasons not listed in the checklist.

_____

_____

Use these as motivators to support your academic goals, achievements, and adventures.

Since that time I have come to understand that for me as well as anyone else, regardless of race, sex, or origin, most limitations are self-set, not God-given. Now, when I see people who have achieved their goals, I remind myself that they, too, started with only a dream. This dream, this goal, is the foundation that every achieved aspiration must rest on in its final manifestation.

Evangela Elliot, student
HERITAGE COLLEGE, TOPPENISH, WASHINGTON

QUICK CHECK

List two questions that you would like to have answered about college.

1. ....
....
....
....

2. ....
....
....
....

Starting college provides a new beginning. Each day that you attend classes and study hard, you will find your dreams developing. Because the college environment is quite different from what you are used to, you may have questions.

▶ Why am I really here?

▶ How can I make the most of college?

▶ How can I keep my motivation strong?

▶ How can I manage my time well enough to balance the academic, personal, and health aspects of my life all at once?

▶ What can I do when I get nervous during tests?

▶ How can I create and maintain strong relationships while in school?

▶ How can I take more effective notes?

▶ How can I read to increase my understanding?

▶ How can I keep my learning skills on target?

▶ What can I do to increase memory retention?

Each of these questions, and many more, will be answered as you work your way through *Claiming Your Victories*. Think of this book as a motivational guide. It will support you as you solve problems, create, strive, take risks, achieve goals, and claim your victories.

Whatever your reasons for being in college, it is no doubt a new experience for you. The challenges and frustrations that you face in the semesters to come will not only help you discover new ideas and knowledge, they will assist you in understanding things about yourself and your own inner strengths. As you work to achieve a college education, you will find that every formula that makes sense to you, every book that becomes part of your personal knowledge, every teacher whose teaching style you understand, will become a personal victory. Enjoy and take pride in each of these accomplishments.

The meaning of victory is different for everyone. Your victory might be as simple as accomplishing the goals or expectations you have for yourself. Victory can also refer to your ability to make the best things happen in life. Or victory may be a developmental quest that changes with each age and stage in your life. Obviously, the victory that you were aiming for at age fourteen is not the same one you are striving to achieve today.

© John Terence Turner/FPG INTERNATIONAL.

© Yellow Dog Productions/THE IMAGE BANK

Create Your Own Victories.

Okay, But Why Did You Come to College?

You probably came to college to increase your likelihood of success. Yet success means different things to different people. What does success mean to you? Maybe success means being able to learn, to think different thoughts, or to make a good living. The following paragraphs explore possible reasons for your presence in college.

To Think New Thoughts

To some, the most important reason for being in college is to learn. An education provides the opportunity to learn and keep on learning. Through classes and exposure to a multitude of ideas, education becomes invaluable. You might say that after college you will never think quite the same way again. Discovering scientific facts, reading literature written in the Roman era, evaluating paintings, participating in discussions with professors, or listening to classical music may cause transformations in thinking. Why? Because exposure to new and different ideas is challenging and exciting, and creates an empowering kind of thinking.

To Increase Income and Chances for Employment

Achieving a college education enables students to find a variety of career-related positions while attaining a higher monetary gain. The fact that you succeeded in college proves to potential employers that you know how to learn and that you can apply the knowledge you gained in various career settings. College increases your writing, speaking, analytical, and mathematical skills, and learning about music, art, and literature helps you become a more well-rounded person. The

POTENTIAL SALARIES FOR ENTRY-LEVEL COLLEGE GRADUATES	
Bachelor's Degree	Salary
Chemical engineering	$43,762
Electrical engineering	40,397
Computer engineering	39,583
Computer science	35,925
Management information systems	38,475
Accounting	35,925
Business	29,784
Liberal arts	28,875

Source: National Association of Colleges and Employers. Adapted from the *Chicago Tribune,* March 16, 1998, Business, p. 2.

courses in your major allow you to learn in-depth information that will support a specific body of knowledge and future career requirements. In many ways, the information learned in college nourishes the life that you want to live in the future.

To Learn More about Yourself

Achieving an education encourages learning about yourself. Each time you find an answer to a problem, create a superb essay, or master new research ideas, you are altering your self-perceptions. Through knowledge comes self-understanding. College provides a chance to increase self-esteem while learning new concepts. The college experience provides a chance to prove your self-worth while exploring new avenues for learning.

To Find Inspiring Jobs after Graduation

College graduates are more likely to find jobs that they enjoy. They often find themselves in positions of responsibility, power, and influence, participating in activities that are based on their interest and education and that are rewarding on a daily basis. Their education provides them with a ticket of entry into positions that might otherwise be closed to them. Attending college is more than getting a degree to get a job. It is an experience that will aid in intellectual growth, emotional change, and behavioral adaptations leading to goal achievement.

To Learn from Others

The people who surround you on your college campus can provide great opportunities to learn. By asking questions and seeking information from classmates, professors, and staff, you can gather a wide array of opinions and experiences that increase your understanding of life issues. Through interactions you will learn of new cultures, new foods, new languages, and new thoughts; this experience enhances your entire college education and your life.

Learning Styles: How Do You Learn Best?

Do you sit in the front row of the lecture hall, listening attentively, writing notes, and remembering 80 percent of what you heard? Do you sit in the middle row, writing down everything on the board, and then study it? Do you write everything on cards, throw the cards on the floor, stomp on them, and then ask yourself questions about each card?

 What Learning Style Works Best for You?

The answer that best describes you correlates to your learning style. When you understand how you learn best, you will need to spend less time studying because you will be studying in the style that is most comfortable and productive for you.

Part of creating victories is understanding yourself and your ability to learn. You will be able to use this knowledge to your advantage to obtain an education and to prepare for a career. You will probably have a favorite learning style, or you may combine various learning styles in different situations. In labs you need to be a hands-on, kinesthetic learner. In lectures, auditory learning skills are crucial. Knowing your learning style and how to use it effectively brings out the best in you. Take the Learning Style Questionnaire on page 6 to find out what kind of learner you might be.

Visual Learning

VISUAL LEARNERS learn best through visual stimuli such as reading, watching, or visually imagining concepts.

Visual learners read, see, or visually imagine concepts in order to recall them. Seeing concepts creates greater understanding and memory retention. Visual learners prefer instructors who write notes on the board or conduct demonstrations. They would rather study their own notes than listen to a lecture or a study group conversation. This is the type of person who may even say, "Please write down what you just said, so that I can understand it better."

The visual learner often speaks in descriptive terms. Directions from a visual learner might be, "Go to the old oak tree and turn right, then go to the red brick schoolhouse and turn left." If you learn best visually, you probably enjoy reading and examining graphs, drawings, visual aids, and diagrams. You may also learn more from demonstrations and step-by-step diagrams written on the board than from lecture-oriented classes.

Auditory Learning

AUDITORY LEARNERS learn best through hearing.

Auditory learners grasp and comprehend information extensively through hearing. For example, knowledge levels are increased by reading aloud notes or assignments. Conversations increase the knowledge level of the auditory learner. This is the type of person who will listen attentively in class when the instructor lectures but loses interest when concepts are written on the board with no discussion. If you learn best as an auditory learner, then you probably prefer discussions, lectures, study groups, and recitation.

Kinesthetic Learning

KINESTHETIC LEARNERS learn best through action and hands-on activities.

Kinesthetic learners master information best through activity or hands-on experience. Handling and touching increase learning. Some kinesthetic learners, for example, cannot tell you a friend's telephone number without first punching out the numbers on an imaginary phone in front of them. The activity of pretending to dial a phone provides memory cues to stored information. For kinesthetic learners, actions stimulate understanding and memory. This is the type of person who might sit in a computer lecture and be very confused. Once the theory can be implemented in a computer lab, great understanding takes place. Kinesthetic learners learn best with tasks that are hands-on (laboratories, mechanics, computers, cooking, simulations). If you are a kinesthetic learner, you probably prefer recording and writing information, and correlating what you learn in class to true-life situations.

Some students find that they do not have one dominant learning style; instead they rely on all three. Whether you are primarily a visual, an auditory, or a kinesthetic learner, understanding is increased through analysis and critical thinking. Questioning, wondering, pondering, thinking, and rethinking enhance learning in all learning styles. Critical thinkers do not accept concepts at face value; they

LEARNING STYLE QUESTIONNAIRE

Answer this questionnaire to gather an introductory understanding of your learning style. Mark the answer that best describes you.

1. I learn best when
   a. I can see a diagram or description of the concept.
   b. I hear the concept presented on tape or in lecture.
   c. I can become actively involved in the concept.

2. I prefer
   a. to learn from instructors who use a computer in the classroom to show concepts from the Internet.
   b. to listen to a lecture rather than read the text.
   c. lab experiments.

3. I like classrooms in which I can
   a. sit in the front row so that I can see everything.
   b. clearly hear the instructor.
   c. maintain my attention level through hands-on-experience.

4. I like group activities in the classroom because
   a. I can see different responses written to the instructor's questions.
   b. I can hear different viewpoints.
   c. I can become more involved in the learning environment.

5. I usually like
   a. reading an assignment.
   b. listening to my classmates summarize readings rather than being involved in group activities.
   c. in-class assignments that involve a lot of activities.

6. I like to learn by
   a. seeing.
   b. hearing.
   c. becoming active in the learning process.

7. Test taking is easier for me when I can
   a. visualize where the answer to the question was in the text.
   b. prepare by studying with others and hear them orally repeating concepts that we need to know.
   c. write potential test questions down and answer them in a written format.

8. When studying I would much rather
   a. see a movie or watch a distance learning seminar than hear an audiotape.
   b. listen to a lecture or discussion than work in a lab.
   c. participate in a lab assignment than read a textbook assignment.

9. My philosophy on learning is
   a. if I listen attentively to a lecture, I will understand it.
   b. if I see a diagram explaining the lecture, my comprehension increases.
   c. if I can take a concept that I need to learn for class and turn it into a song, I learn it better (especially when I sing it repeatedly in the shower).

10. Comprehension is increased when
    a. the professor writes down an explanation of a difficult subject.
    b. I listen to a study tape that I created while I do the dishes or work in the garden.
    c. I jump rope and practice the terms for the class at the same time.

11. Learning is a continuous lifelong process that is made easier by
    a. reading.
    b. lectures.
    c. laboratory assignments.

If most of your responses were "a," you may be a visual learner; "b," you may be an auditory learner; "c," you may be a kinesthetic learner.

want to know more through introspection. Those who take time to reflect on readings and to understand more completely the ideas to which they are exposed will increase their learning skills no matter which learning style is their primary one.

Right-Brain, Left-Brain Learning

Another factor that relates to learning style is brain-dominance theory. Each hemisphere of the brain controls certain parts of your personality, thinking, and behavior. By understanding if you are right-brain dominant or left-brain dominant, you will be more aware of your learning and working patterns. Fill out the Right-Brain/Left-Brain Questionnaire below to find out what your dominant learning mode might be.

QUICK CHECK

Do you think you are a right-brain or a left-brain thinker? Use examples to explain your answer.

....

....

....

....

....

....

....

Source: Adapted from Nancy Lightfoot Matte and Susan Hilary Green Henderson, *Success Your Style!* © 1995 Wadsworth Publishing Company. Adapted from James Shepherd, *College Study Skills,* Sixth Edition. Copyright © 1998 by Houghton Mifflin Company.

RIGHT-BRAIN/LEFT-BRAIN QUESTIONNAIRE

The following is a list of statements. Mark the ones that best describe you.

1. When I study I
   a. take a logical, problem-solving approach to understanding concepts presented in lecture.
   b. daydream and think about information presented in lectures.

2. When playing music I
   a. read it.
   b. recognize and remember melodies and musical chords.

3. When studying, my desk is usually
   a. organized.
   b. scattered with many things.

4. I respond well to
   a. facts.
   b. feelings.

5. I take pride in understanding
   a. verbal communication very well.
   b. nonverbal behaviors and emotions very well.

6. I like to
   a. think rationally based on facts, reasons, and logic.
   b. think intuitively based on premonitions, feelings, and emotions.

7. I like to
   a. think and then act.
   b. act and then think.

8. I like to
   a. plan and schedule my time.
   b. just let things happen; things will get done eventually.

9. I often
   a. work on one project until it is finished.
   b. jump from project to project.

10. I like to
    a. listen, reflect, and then respond to others.
    b. express my feelings and reactions without totally understanding the whole situation.

If most of your responses were "a," you are probably a left-brain thinker; "b," you are probably a right-brain thinker.

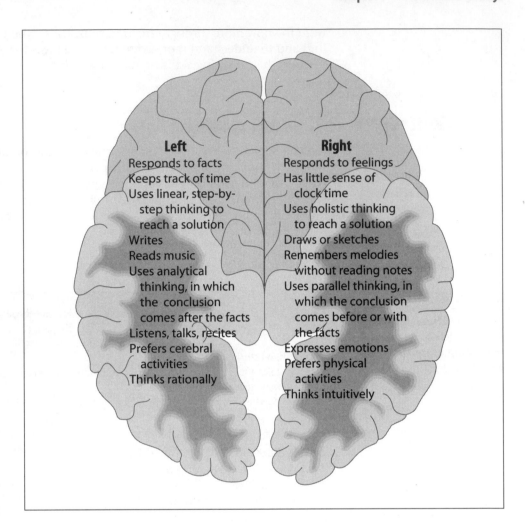

Characteristics attributed to the left and right sides of the brain.
Source: Reprinted by permission from *Success Your Style!* by Nancy Lightfoot Matte and Susan Hilary Green Henderson. © 1995 Wadsworth Publishing Company.

Those who are LEFT-BRAIN DOMINANT are logical, serious, knowledgeable, linear in thinking, structured, organized, and rational.

Are you a left-brain learner? Those who are left-brain dominant are often logical, serious, knowledgeable, structured, organized, and rational. They often think in a linear, organized fashion. Sporadic unorganized thoughts are foreign to them. They enjoy learning facts, analyzing in a concrete format, and maintaining a sense of order. They like to read music, use names to describe and define things, and respond to lists. Left-brain dominance encourages fact-oriented thinking and reasoning. Left-brain learners are more likely to create and follow time management charts, have a neat study area, and finish projects ahead of time.

Those who are RIGHT-BRAIN DOMINANT are intuitive; have little sense of time; enjoy music, clutter, and creative thinking; make decisions based on hunches and emotions; and use holistic thinking.

Are you a right-brain learner? Right-brain-dominant people respond to feelings, are intuitive, have little sense of time, and use parallel thinking (the conclusions come before or with the facts). They do not mind clutter and are creative in thinking processes. They like to be playful, intuitive, and spontaneous; they enjoy drawing and doing physical activities. They often make decisions based on abstract thinking, hunches, and emotions, or on "the whole picture" (Matte, 1995; Shepherd, 1998; Ferrett, 1997).

If you can learn to use both sides of your brain, you may find that you can expand your skills, thinking processes, and formats for organization. By striving to acknowledge and empower skills from both cerebral sides, you are opening yourself to the creation of new study strategies and lifelong learning skills.

EXERCISE

How Do You Learn Best?

The purpose of this exercise is to correlate your learning style and brain dominance to effective study strategies.

When you took the Learning Style Questionnaire, did you discover that you are a visual, auditory, or kinesthetic learner? Are there times when you use all three learning styles?

When you took the Right-Brain/Left-Brain Questionnaire, did you discover that you are a left-brain or a right-brain thinker?

Discuss five specific ways that you could improve your study habits based on your new understanding of learning styles and brain-dominance theory.

1. _____

2. _____

3. _____

4. _____

5. _____

Take Charge of Your Education

Beyond understanding your learning style preference or the relationship between brain dominance and studying, it is also important to understand other factors that you can control when guiding your college decisions.

Step Inside Your College Community

Research shows that the more you connect with your college community, the more successful you will be throughout your academic life. By learning about the people, departments, services, and clubs at your college, it becomes easier to fit in and feel like a part of the college community. That is why each chapter in this book includes a Step Inside . . . section that describes various resources on campus that have been created to support your college success. By getting to know more about your college campus, your comfort level will increase, and little successes will build into college victories.

Ask Questions and Seek Answers

When things seem confusing, look for answers. Take responsibility and time to find solutions. Colleges are set up to answer questions and to help you become successful. The more you ask, the wiser you will be. There is no reason for you to walk around the hallways mumbling to yourself in frustration; instead, go into any office and ask your question. If you are in the wrong place, be assured that staff, faculty, or other students will direct you to the right place.

Keep All Papers

Keep *all* papers that you receive from the college. Whether they are graded assignments, financial aid forms, or registration guidelines, keep them in a folder with an appropriate title (e.g., English, loan forms, scholarship papers, registration forms). This will promote organization and prevent tie-ups when you need to speak with Financial Aid Office or Registrar Office staff.

Homework, Tests, Projects.   Keep all papers handed back to you by your instructor. You can study them for future tests and, in the case of errors, learn the correct information. Secondarily, such papers may serve as evidence if you believe the instructor has graded you incorrectly. If you receive a report card with a grade that you think could be mistaken, make an appointment to discuss it with the instructor. Most colleges have grade change deadlines; look in your student handbook to see what the policy is for your school.

Financial Aid Papers.   You may receive many financial aid papers. Keep all of them. Find out the name of your financial aid advisor and post it in your address book or on your refrigerator for easy access. Pay special attention to payment dates; mark them on a calendar so that you will not have to pay late fees.

Go to Class

There is a direct correlation between grades and attendance. The more faithful your attendance, the higher your grades. If you miss class, you miss not only the lecture and discussion that will aid in your understanding of concepts but also pop quizzes, homework assignments, or in-class assignments. Missing any or all of these activities can lead to lower grades.

If you have to miss a class, check your student handbook for the attendance policy. Many instructors will list their attendance rules in the syllabus; check it to see if you are supposed to call them if you will not be in class.

Become Informed

Be aware of all policies. Do you know where you can park without being towed? Do you know what prerequisites you need before signing up for a specific course? Do you know what hours the library is open? By reading materials provided to you and by reviewing the handbook and the catalogue, you will be an informed student. The information that you learn now will prevent misinformation and confusion later.

Check Deadlines

When can you withdraw from a course without a penalty? When is the last date to add a course? When do you take proficiency exams? When do you have to make housing payments? Each deadline, if missed, will cause hassles or cost money. Get a calendar and mark deadlines on it now so you can be aware of them for the whole semester.

Budget Your Money

How much does it cost to live? List the amount that you spend on rent, utilities, phone, food, transportation, insurance, entertainment, clothing, laundry, and miscellaneous items. Add your expenses and compare them to your income.

| AVERAGE MONTHLY EXPENSES OF STUDENTS LIVING AWAY FROM HOME ||
Item	Cost
Rent or dormitory fees	$ 248
Utilities and phone	96
Food	224
Transportation	15
Insurance	38
Entertainment	90
Clothing	101
Laundry and toiletries	20
Miscellaneous	—
Total	$ 832

Source: U.S. Department of Labor. 1995 Consumer Expenditures Survey for the "Under 25" Age Group. Adapted from Anne Nelson, "Juggling the Costs of Living Away from Home." *Class of '99 Futures,* Spring 1998.

Create a budget based on these figures. By figuring out how much you spend monthly, you can more easily understand where your money goes and curtail your spending. To get some idea, look at the chart above that shows the average monthly expenses of students living away from home (Nelson, 1998).

QUICK CHECK

List the amounts that you pay for items mentioned in the average expenses chart. How do your costs differ?

....

....

....

....

....

....

....

Cut Costs Creatively.   Find ways to spend less money. Locate banks that do not charge high service fees. Buy soap, razors, and shampoo in bulk. Try to find grocery stores that have double-coupon days so that you can save twice the amount on groceries.

If you feel you must eat out (eating out can destroy a budget), use coupons to reduce the price of your meal. Find restaurants that provide large servings and split one order with a friend. Reduce the number of times you eat out (e.g., try to eat out only once a month). If you have chosen the food plan at your dorm, eat in the dorm, not in restaurants, as much as possible (Nelson, 1998).

Check with Student Services to see if they have discount coupons for amusement parks, movies, concerts, and restaurants. Use public transportation, ride your bicycle, or walk to save wear and tear on your car as well as gas money. Check the car pool board to see who lives in your area and might be interested in sharing a ride. Before you buy, stop and think, "Do I have the money? If I do not, I will not buy it." "Can I live without this for a week? If so, I do not need to buy it now." Be careful that impulsive buying does not cause you to break your budget (Nelson, 1998; Flood, 1998).

Credit Cards Can Become Your Worst Enemy.   Be cautious with credit cards. You may decide that you need one for emergencies. If so, that is all it should be used for. Often, credit card companies come to college campuses to lure students to apply for credit cards. Think about your budget; if you start to place charges on your new credit card, how will you pay them off? If most of your salary is now allotted for survival, do you think you will be able to pay your monthly credit card bill at 15 or 21 percent interest? Sometimes, credit card companies will give you a T-shirt, a water bottle, or a candy bar when you fill out the application. If you really want a T-shirt or a candy bar, buy it yourself instead; it will be less costly. Many students report that they signed up for a credit card and used it for anything they wanted—pizza, a new shirt, greeting cards, or going to amusement parks. They realized, too late, that paying off the credit card bill was going to be difficult and painful because the interest kept accruing and their credit card debt never seemed to end (Flood, 1998).

To pay off credit card debt, you might have to work more hours. This work time will take away from your study time. You may also find that worrying about

Credit card purchases can
become your worst enemy.
By Ruth Flanigan.

how to pay it off will prevent you from being able to focus on studying. By making the choice to prevent credit card debt, you will be able to spend more time and focused energy on your studies and academic achievements.

Finding ways to take charge of your education will ensure your success in college. To continue your success, it is important to find ways to keep your motivation high.

Find Ways to Stay Motivated

Motivation exists within you and supports your desire to turn dreams into reality. It is nonmeasurable, yet it is one of the more powerful psychological factors that help you attain your goals. As you attend college, motivation directs how you handle classes, attendance, homework, tests, or relationships.

EXTRINSIC MOTIVATORS are
factors outside you that prompt
you to strive for goals.

There are extrinsic and intrinsic motivators. Extrinsic motivators come from outside of yourself: grades, pay, material rewards, social pressures. If a reward is important to you, it can be a great motivator. For example, if you have two kids, have lost your job, and are attending school, it will be extrinsically rewarding to find a job. It may even be more rewarding to find a position that will support you and your family and allow you to advance yourself through your education.

INTRINSIC MOTIVATORS are
factors inside you that prompt
you to strive for goals.

Intrinsic motivators come from inside yourself. Examples include enjoyment of work, pride in self-achievement, learning for the sake of learning. Intrinsic motivators exist at a feeling level. This feeling level can be so strong that once you make up your mind to achieve a specific goal, no outside influence will stop you.

An important part of claiming your victories is understanding what motivates you and how that motivation relates to your goals. Think about which intrinsic and extrinsic motivators are important to you. If you think that the most important motivation in college is to get good grades so that you can get a good job that pays well, you will be in possession of knowledge that is externally motivating (extrinsic motivation). On the other hand, if you know that the most important motivator for you is the enjoyment of learning, then you know that intrinsic motivation is important to you. There are times that you may be motivated by both intrinsic and extrinsic motivators.

Identifying factors that motivate you can help you keep on track in attaining your goals when you are struggling or frustrated. Knowing what motivates you is the key to staying motivated, even in the roughest situations. Why? Because each time the going gets tough, you can remind yourself of what you are working for and why it is so important. This reminder can serve as a motivator in itself. It can be useful to you whenever you begin to question your motivational level.

Many times, intrinsic and extrinsic motivators are in conflict. You may want to be a college graduate (extrinsic motivation), but *hate* spending time studying in the library on a beautiful day (intrinsic motivation). The question in this motivational conflict is which motivational factor will win? By thinking about your motivators and clarifying them, you may be able to create a clearer understanding of yourself and what helps keep you motivated. This process will aid you in achieving your goals and claiming your victories—large or small.

To understand the concept of intrinsic and extrinsic motivation further, answer the following questions. Mark "yes" if the statement describes you very well, and mark "no" if it does not.

Yes	No	
		Do you make decisions in life based on what your friends, spouse, or family tell you to do?
		Does what you see or hear in the media affect your goals?
		Do you have a difficult time making decisions and look toward someone else to help you make up your mind?
		Are you motivated by the events around you? (For example, you plan on studying all night for your anthropology test; then your friends ask you to go out for pizza. Do you go?)
		Do you make a decision and when someone tells you your decision was wrong, change your thinking to conform to his or her opinion?
		When things go wrong, do you project your anger on others? (For example, when you fail your test, do you blame it on the teaching style of your instructor?)

QUICK CHECK

List one extrinsic and one intrinsic factor that motivates you.

1. ....

....

....

2. ....

....

....

If you answered yes to most of the questions, your motivation may be based on extrinsic motivators. Your decisions are based more on the factors and people around you than on the feelings and opinions that spring from within you. You may often value others' opinions more than your own. You may also blame others when things go wrong rather than look inside yourself to see what part you might have played in the problem.

If you answered no to most of the questions, then you are more likely a person who experiences intrinsic motivation. You make decisions based on your own perceptions, feelings, and reactions. You try to prevent the outside environment from controlling you. You acknowledge your feelings, and you acknowledge outside factors, but your decisions are based on your perception of the best action for the specific situation. You also realize that your perception of the negative events in your life, over which you have no control, can be dealt with only through understanding. You might not be able to change the event, but you can still keep your perceptions in check. You realize that worry and negative thoughts do not change difficult events, that it is your reaction to those events that can decrease their stressful impact and increase your motivation to prevent them from interfering with your successes.

No one can give you motivation, and no one can take it away. Motivation lies within you. When you say, "I am just not motivated," it is important to remember that you are the only one who can rejuvenate motivation.

Diversity

How Would You Define Diversity?

Diversity exists around you. No matter where you are or what you are doing, there are always those who are different from you. Whether you are in class, in your community, or watching TV, you probably note differences in others. Not just skin color, body size, or the earring in an eyebrow—diversity is more than that. Diversity comprises all differences: personality, gender, interests, attitudes, food, religious beliefs, and more. Diversity champions individual differences. Part of learning in college is being exposed to different ideas, thoughts, and attitudes. When encountering differences, make it an opportunity to learn, adapt, and possibly alter your own opinion.

Sometimes students voice concern about being different from the majority of the class. They feel they are older, younger, or culturally or physically different. They are concerned, for example, that they will not be able to learn as quickly as younger students or that their language or physical barriers will prevent them from learning. In reality, students who see themselves in this light often experience high degrees of motivation and excel academically.

Formal institutional support systems are great. But do not forget to create and maintain friendships while in college. Your school is a good place to meet people from all over the world. Not only is it a great cultural experience but the support you receive from friends is often unmatched. Who understands your frustration in a class better than someone else in the same class?

By accepting differences, considering new ideas, and evaluating others' contributions based on their thoughts and originality, you will experience how powerful diversity can be. We live in a global village. This village allows for exploration of differences while considering new perspectives that empower you to grow, change, and learn. Sometimes, learning from others is just as powerful as book learning.

Reprinted with permission by Gary Hoskins.

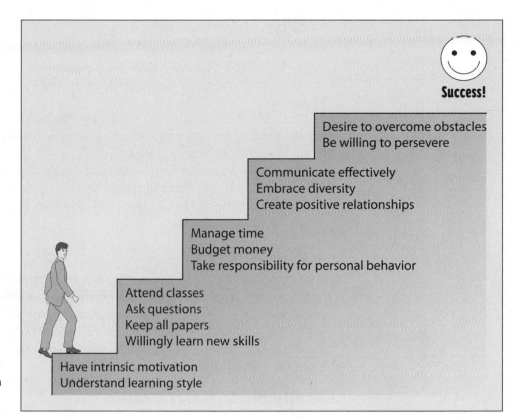

Success!

Desire to overcome obstacles
Be willing to persevere

Communicate effectively
Embrace diversity
Create positive relationships

Manage time
Budget money
Take responsibility for personal behavior

Attend classes
Ask questions
Keep all papers
Willingly learn new skills

Have intrinsic motivation
Understand learning style

A student's success is often a step-by-step process that includes many factors.

The College Challenge

There is no doubt that your college experience will be a challenge. It is a time of learning, exploring, and creating a new aspect of life. Know that no matter how tough it becomes, you can make it. By succeeding at college you are building your future. Much of what you learn here will be useful to you throughout your personal and professional life. So go ahead . . . take the challenge. It might be difficult, but you will not regret it.

Step Inside . . . Your College Campus

Take a step inside the various offices on your college campus. The college has set up services for you as a support to your academic endeavors. Do not pass by offices and wonder what they are about; go in, visit, and ask questions. The more you meet people on your campus and speak with them, the more you will feel like a part of the college community. The following is a sampling of resources available to you at your college. Search these resources out, ask questions, find out who else can help you be successful at your school.

Each college has different services, and yours may have names different from those presented here. Most of the services available are also listed in your Student Handbook. Do not allow yourself to wander around lost as a new student. College staff and faculty want to help you.

Faculty

Most instructors joined the teaching profession to share knowledge and help you learn. Tap into that knowledge by asking questions in class, and if you need additional information, make an appointment to see them after class or during office hours.

Teaching assistants (faculty assistants) may also be available for tutoring. Ask a faculty member or the secretary in the academic office about the availability of tutoring from the instructor's assistant.

Remember to ask for help before you start doing below-average work. Do not wait until midterms or finals to obtain help. It will be easier to be successful in the course if you do not fall too far behind. As soon as you receive a grade that you feel is unsatisfactory, seek help.

Student Services

Most campuses have a department that is set up to serve you. Make sure that you find it, and ask what services the staff members can offer. They may be able to provide information to you on campus counseling, part-time jobs, housing, student organizations, and community services. If you feel lost when you arrive at college, seek out this department. It may be the support system that you need to make yourself feel more comfortable on a new campus.

Academic Support Center

Although the name of this center might be different on various campuses, most colleges have one. It often offers tutoring, study skills seminars, and support to each student. It may also provide support, guidance, and learning strategies to the English-as-a-Second-Language student, the physically challenged student, or the student with learning disabilities.

QUICK CHECK

What is your advisor's name? room number? phone number?

....

....

....

Academic Advising

Advisors can make sure you are on the right track. They can help you determine if your academic load is too heavy, help you decide about changing your major, or provide suggestions on whom you can see for additional tutoring. Each campus has an advising office where you can obtain help in creating class schedules, choosing classes, or planning your college career. Staff members will provide information on the number of credits and courses you will need to graduate. They will also explain the prerequisites or requirements needed for each course to make the scheduling of your classes much easier. If you have questions about the level of courses that you are taking, or feel that you are taking too many courses, contact your advisor. Your advisor's name and phone number will be listed in the college catalogue.

Study Groups

Create a study group and meet with it regularly (at least once a week). Study groups can provide support in studying, getting over loneliness, finding your way around campus, and adjusting to a new environment. Do not underestimate the power of study groups. They provide the structure, knowledge, and support needed to achieve college goals. They will make copies of the notes you missed when you were sick. They will push you to study harder when you want to give up. Group members will listen when things get rough and explain perplexing concepts until they seem simple.

Study groups are a key factor in college success.
© Susie Fitzhugh.

Study groups increase learning power. When you have four people reviewing the same subject, you learn faster than you can on your own. Another advantage is that you can help each other study because of individual strengths and weaknesses within the group. You might be great at math and not great at English, but another group member may be good at English and not good at math. Study groups compensate for each members' weaknesses while capitalizing on the group's strengths.

Besides, it is much more fun to study in a group. The group motivating factor is usually stronger than individual motivation. There may be times when you will not feel like studying, yet you need to. When a member of the study group calls you and says, "We are all at McDonald's studying. Where are you?" it may give you the motivation to get out of bed and get moving. Group members can push you gently and quiz you into learning material. Reach out to others and form a study group; the benefits will be never ending.

Career Counseling

Staff members in this office can help you find a full-time, co-op, or part-time job. They can offer you advice on career opportunities before and after graduation. They can also help you create a dynamic résumé and teach you appropriate interviewing skills. The placement office may provide you with opportunities to meet with company recruiters or schedule job interviews for you when you are close to graduation.

Financial Aid Office

QUICK CHECK

Write the name, room number, and phone number of your financial aid counselor.

....

....

....

You will want to visit this office when you have questions about scholarships, school loans, or grants. The staff in this office will work with you to help you find financial assistance. Before you drop out of school because of money problems, be sure to visit the Financial Aid Office. The staff has the expertise to help you evaluate your financial situation more objectively.

Be sure to look around campus for support systems, because they do exist. It is up to you to use them. Your first college semester can be wonderful, but it can also be confusing and overwhelming. By making the right contacts, you may find that the answers to your problems may be simpler than you think.

Internet Exercise

Access the Internet and look up the Web site for your college. If you are not sure how to do this, ask your instructor for help. Locate the following information:

1. Who was the founder of your college or university? What year was it established?

2. What are three curricula in which you could major?

3. Name two instructors who teach at your school (who are not currently teaching your classes). List three interesting things to know about them.

4. Find out what the last date is to withdraw from a class for this semester.

5. Record the library hours for Friday night, Saturday, and Sunday.

Role Play Calvin

Break into groups of four or five, and read aloud the setting and role play. Your task is to create the ending of this role play through discussion and collaboration in your group. You may change the dialogue and add new characters. Your role play conclusion should demonstrate that you have reflected on the character's perspective and his circumstances. Then, act the role play out for the class. After each group has acted out its role play, discuss the questions that follow.

Setting: *Calvin and Jeff, in their dorm rooms at their respective colleges, are talking on the phone. They are brothers.*

Calvin has just turned eighteen. It is the first semester of his freshman year at a large state university and his first time living away from home. The school is more than 600 miles from his home. None of his high school friends are at the college. Although Calvin is very close to his family, he could not wait to leave for school. His girlfriend Candy attends a college near his hometown and still goes out with many of Calvin's friends.

Jeff is in his third year of college. He attends a small university about 200 miles from home. He is active in the college drama club and has joined Amnesty International.

Calvin: [*To himself*] I'm going crazy out here. It's so lonely. My roommate is never around. I would love to call home, but then they'll think I am homesick. A guy can't be homesick. I guess I could call Jeff. I hope he doesn't make fun of me. Maybe I shouldn't call. This is the pits. I've got to talk to someone. [*Calls Jeff*]

Jeff: Hello.

Calvin: Jeff, it's me, Calvin.

Jeff: I knew it was you when I answered the phone. I have lived with that voice for eighteen years. What's up, little brother?

Calvin: Don't start, Jeff. I hate it when you act superior.

Jeff: It's not acting. I merely am.

Calvin: Stop! I'm not in the mood.

Jeff: What mood are you in? . . . Hey, are you still there?

Calvin: I'm going nuts here. There's no one around to talk to. The school is so big. The only time anyone talks to you is when they bump into you. And then they say, "Watch where you're going!"

Jeff: Yeah, well big schools are like that at first. You've just got to meet a few people. That's all.

Calvin: To top it off, Candy has not called or written to me. I bet she's going out with my friend Chuck. He was always with her when I was not around.

Jeff: Hey, guy. You have got to stop thinking like that.

Calvin: I wanted this freedom. Now, I hate it. I even thought about calling Mom and Dad to tell them I have changed my mind about this school and that I want to come home.

Jeff: Are you nuts? They would kill you. You know how much tuition money they would lose? You have got to work this out.

Calvin: I'm just lost out here. What can I do?

Continue this dialogue. Use Jeff's character to help Calvin through the transition.

Questions

1. What issues are bothering Calvin?

2. How could he help himself? What campus services could he use?

3. What issues are you confronting? What services could you use?

Review

This review is correlated with the objectives at the start of the chapter. One way to study Chapter 1 is to look at the objectives, write down everything you learned about each one, and then compare your notes to this review.

1. *Each positive college experience is a personal victory.* Starting college is the start of a new adventure where you will be in charge of claiming academic victories.

2. *By asking and answering questions, you will more clearly understand your reasons for attending college.*

3. *Understanding your most effective learning style aids you in understanding the best ways to study, take notes, and prepare for college.*

   Visual learning: You learn best when you see, read, or visually imagine concepts. You prefer lecturers who use visuals and overheads or who write on the board.

   Auditory learning: You understand information better when you hear it. You learn best through discussions, study groups, and lectures.

   Kinesthetic learning: Using hands-on experiences is the way you like to learn. You learn best with tasks that use your hands, including experiments in labs, and mechanical and computer assignments.

4. *Each hemisphere of the brain controls certain parts of your thinking and behavior and therefore correlates directly to your study strategies.*

   Left-brained: You are logical, serious, knowledgeable, linear in thinking, structured, organized, and rational. You like to learn facts, analyze information in a concrete format, have a sense of order, like to read music, respond to lists, and are thought-oriented.

   Right-brained: You are intuitive, have little sense of time, enjoy playing music without notes, and enjoy clutter and creative thinking. You make decisions based on hunches and emotions and use holistic thinking.

5. *You can take charge of your education.* Step inside your college community to ask questions and seek answers. Keep all papers, join a study group, visit your advisor, go to class, read college handbooks and catalogues, check deadlines, budget your money. Be cautious when using credit cards. Find ways to stay motivated.

6. *Motivation is what moves you toward your goals.* Everyone is motivated by different factors; it is important for you to identify the major motivations in your life.

   Intrinsic motivators: Intrinsic motivators come from within you and exist at a feeling level. Pride in self-achievement and desire to learn are examples. You feel that control in your life comes from inside of you.

   Extrinsic motivators: Extrinsic motivators come from outside of you. Examples are praise from your instructor, paychecks, and high grades. You feel that control in your life comes from outside of you.

7. *Identify campus resources:* Scout out your campus for resources that can help you be successful in college. Find out where faculty offices, student services, academic support centers, financial aid offices, and advising centers are located. Also find out what each one can do to help you and other students.

Critical Thinking and Problem Solving

CHAPTER 2

OBJECTIVES

By the end of this chapter, you will be able to . . .

1. Understand what critical thinking is and that it is the foundation for questioning, analyzing, and problem solving.

2. Understand that critical thinking often leads to new solutions and new perceptions.

3. Become a critical thinker.

4. Understand that problem solving is the ability to work out solutions creatively.

5. Know and implement steps to problem solving.

6. Understand that there are times when failure is okay.

CRITICAL THINKING CHECKLIST

The purpose of the following checklist is to help you diagnose your ability to think critically.

Check the appropriate answer:

1. Do you usually believe what you read?   YES _____ NO _____

2. Do you usually accept as fact what professors or mentors say?   YES _____ NO _____

3. When you study, do you often look beyond words for different meanings?   YES _____ NO _____

4. Do you ask questions to further your understanding?   YES _____ NO _____

5. Do you like to ponder information beyond its superficial meaning?   YES _____ NO _____

6. Are you open to new ideas?   YES _____ NO _____

7. Do you like to discuss alternative solutions to problems with others?   YES _____ NO _____

8. Do you let your mind wander when solving problems?   YES _____ NO _____

9. When solving problems, do you sometimes let intuition guide decisions?   YES _____ NO _____

10. Do you ask "Why?" or "Is this true?" as you read?   YES _____ NO _____

If you are a successful critical thinker, your answers to questions 3–10 would be yes, and your answers to questions 1 and 2 would be no. Write about your critical thinking skills that still need improvement.

_____

_____

_____

_____

_____

_____

A n educated man is one whose mind is widened out, so that
he can take broad views, instead of being narrow-minded;
so that he can see the different sides of a question, or at least can
know that all questions have different sides. An educated man is
one who has the power of patient thinking; who can fasten his
mind on a subject, and hold it there while he pleases; who can
keep looking at a subject, till he sees into it and sees through
it. . . . Again, an educated man is one who has sound judgment,
who knows how to reason to right conclusions, and so to argue
as to convince others that he is right.

John Broadus
A Treatise on the Preparation and Delivery of Sermons, 1870

CRITICAL THINKING is a process in which questioning, challenging, dissecting, and problem solving are important tools for active learning.

QUICK CHECK

How would you define critical thinking? Provide a specific example.

Broadus felt that individuals need to see different sides of questions, think patiently, look at a subject until it is understood, use sound judgment, and know how to reason until a correct solution is found. In the 1880s these traits indicated an educated man; today we call people who possess these characteristics critical thinkers. Critical thinking is the ability to dissect information by way of reasoning, questioning, challenging facts, problem solving, and rethinking. These processes allow you to make sense out of confusion, to understand the difference between opinion and fact, and to challenge old thoughts in order to create newer, more effective ones. Critical thinking is a sequential process that plays an important role in such activities as computing mathematical equations, solving roommate conflicts, teaching AIDS prevention to teenagers, or finding one's way around a college campus.

Critical thinking is a process that encourages you to question and wonder before you act or assume; it precedes actions and decisions. College is the perfect place to rekindle your ability to question, wonder, and ask why as you rediscover the child in you. This process enhances the desire to wonder about and question information. Like a child that sees a rock in a yard and cannot leave it unexamined, you should not refuse the inclination to turn over knowledge until it is understood from your perspective. When you were three years old, *why* was a major part of your vocabulary: "Why do fish swim?" "Why does mom have to work today?" "Why does a dog wag its tail?" This wonder often fades with age, yet it is this very simple questioning, analyzing, and rethinking that is essential for college success. After you ask a question, do not accept the first answer that comes to mind. Instead, seek alternative answers. Critical thinking involves stretching your thoughts before settling on a definitive answer.

Becoming a Critical Thinker

Think Differently

Why is critical thinking an essential learning tool? Because it forces you to question what you hear, see, or experience. Effective critical thinkers learn to evaluate everything they perceive. Consider the endless barrage of information received

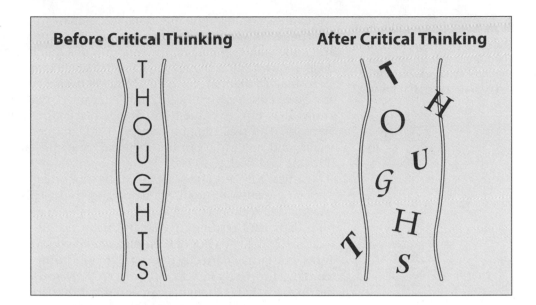

The foundation of critical thinking is created by stretching thought into a new form.

daily, ranging from your family's opinions of what you should do with your life, to TV advertisements that lure you to order a pizza, to a biology instructor who tells you that a turkey did not get its name because it comes from Turkey (in fact, it comes from Mexico), but that the bird's name came from the call "turk, turk, turk" (*1000 More Questions and Answers,* 1989). The processes you use to sort out the family's opinions, the TV's proclamations, and the instructor's remarks on turkeys involve critical thinking.

Question and Challenge Facts

Many educators want students to use critical thinking skills to enhance their knowledge rather than to accept passively all information as fact. If you hear or read something that you disagree with, do not automatically suppress your own opinion and assume that others' opinions are right. Often, differences of opinion provide great insight. Allow your mind to wander, question, analyze, and challenge.

Thinking differently creates powerful results.
University of Wisconsin—Oshkosh.

QUICK CHECK

State a fact or theory learned in class. Break it down into two significant subquestions. What did you learn from this process?

....

....

....

....

....

....

....

....

....

Express and reiterate questions in different ways. If a question is too vague, too trivial, or too difficult, you may miss its purpose. Without purpose, learning and understanding may escape your grip. If a question seems too overwhelming, break it down into subquestions. Several smaller, more specific questions are easier to analyze than one long, complicated, indirect one. Make sure your questions are clear, concise, significant, and relevant. Trivial questions bring superficial knowledge. Effective questions change perceptions and help new ideas emerge. Never give up searching for answers to tough questions. Through systematic research and analysis, learning increases, and substantial answers can be found (Browne and Keeley, 1994).

Critical thinkers also search for facts supported by data. Their thinking is supported by evidence, proof, statistics, and truth. This is often balanced by using imagination to understand in different ways the material being presented in lectures, labs, and reading. If your instructor claims that farmers can forecast the weather by the behavior of their pigs, would you consider this fact or opinion? In Texas, one farmer correctly forecast eight rainstorms out of ten, while the local meteorologist correctly forecast only one (*1000 More Questions and Answers,* 1989). On hearing this, what thoughts come to mind that challenge the validity of this information? (For instance, ten pigs is a small sample; has further research been done in this area? What pig behaviors let the farmer know that rain was on its way? Did the farmer condition his pigs to act in weather-predicting ways?) By looking for evidence, questioning research methods, and asking for sources of information, you create a newer, unbiased point of view.

Open Your Mind

QUICK CHECK

List two examples where you use objective, nonbiased thinking when studying.

1. ....

2. ....

Seek to understand and learn without bias. By opening your mind to controversy, you learn the value of different thoughts and perceptions. Choose to debate differing viewpoints; disagreements feed new thought. If you listen to someone who is passionate on a topic, you will not be able to stop yourself from learning. Through evaluation of the evidence behind the claims, you will attain new knowledge. Embrace this new information, and allow it to feed your college learning experiences (Beatrice, 1993).

Discuss Issues with Others

Others may discover solutions that have never occurred to you. Involving others in the creative thinking process allows you to consider many ideas and perceptions instead of just your own isolated viewpoint. It is a great way to incorporate the

Searching for facts supported by evidence, discussion, and critical thinking is the foundation of learning in college labs.
© Susie Fitzhugh.

experiences and knowledge of others into your own. Remember that you are the one who must make the final analysis. Never allow others to talk you into a solution with which you feel uncomfortable.

Anticipate Negative and Positive Implications

When using critical thinking to create conclusions or decisions, prevent unexpected consequences by anticipating the results of your thinking process. Critical thinkers realize that for every action there is a reaction, and they attempt to predict what that is before it occurs without being overly pessimistic or blindly optimistic.

Let Your Mind Wander

Let your mind wander. By removing the restraints that prevent creative thinking, you can make discoveries that you never imagined. For example, if you censor thoughts that make you feel confused, it will be difficult to take the next step that forces confusion to evolve into understanding. By allowing yourself to entertain a different view, angle, or perception, new, undiscovered thoughts are realized.

Free association and visualization are tools that encourage critical thinking and creative problem solving. Close your eyes and visualize the problem you are facing. Allow all thoughts and associations to flow freely through your mind. Now, open your eyes and write down everything that you thought about and analyze the information. What did you learn about this problem? What did you learn about yourself? Did you find any new solutions to the problem? This creative process works because you are letting ideas happen naturally instead of consciously monitoring each idea that travels through your mind.

QUICK CHECK

Take thirty seconds and think about a specific problem. Now, use free-writing and record all thoughts on a separate sheet of paper. What did you learn?

Be Intuitive

Trust your gut instincts. Do not let logic get in the way of flexibility and creativity. Logical thinking is important, but sometimes the best critical thinking emerges under the auspices of just "letting it all hang out." Be creative. Do not let logical thinking stunt your imagination or your originality.

You will soon discover that critical thinking is important in everything you do. Creative thinking affects the way you study, manage time and money, read, and solve problems.

Critical thinking includes discussing issues with others.
© Anthony Wood/STOCK BOSTON.

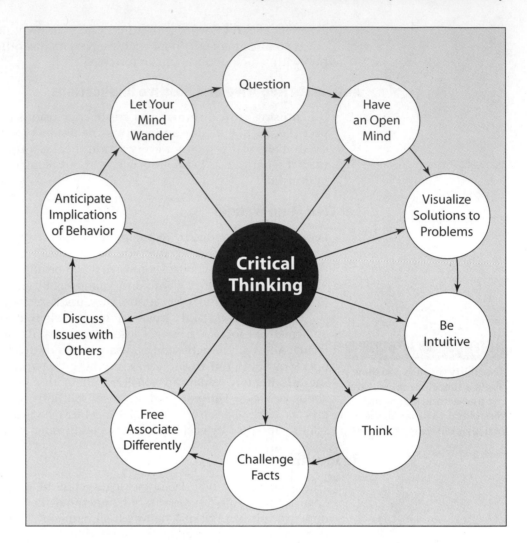

Critical thinking is a continuous process comprising many factors.

Practice Critical Thinking

The purpose of this exercise is to practice critical thinking skills.

1. Choose an article from a magazine or journal and examine it critically by answering the following questions:

   a. What is the view presented by the author?

   _____

   _____

   _____

   _____

   b. Do you agree with the reasoning process used in the article?

   _____

   _____

   _____

c. If you had written the article, what conclusions would you have developed?

_____

_____

d. What questions would you use to understand the information more critically?

_____

_____

e. Provide one concrete example from the article that supports
   your ideas.

_____

_____

2. Choose a TV show and analyze it critically.
a. What message is the show sending?

_____

_____

_____

b. What values or beliefs are promoted by the actors and actresses
   in the show?

_____

_____

c. How do you feel children or elderly people would react to this show?

_____

_____

d. What questions would you ask to understand the plot more clearly?

_____

_____

e. Provide one concrete example from the show that supports
   your ideas.

_____

_____

_____

There is always more than one way to solve a problem. Being able to think of different ways to solve problems gives students the edge. Free-thinking is one of the most important characteristics of these students. Problem solving can make it possible to achieve long-term goals and become successful in any endeavor.

Jennifer Johnston, student
DES MOINES AREA COMMUNITY COLLEGE, ANKENY, IOWA

What Is Problem Solving?

PROBLEM SOLVING is a process that includes finding creative, effective answers to questions, problems, or conflicts.

Problem solving allows you to put all of your critical thinking skills to the test. When problems seem complex, problem solving uses the best thinking. Problem solving correlates with your ability to work out solutions to problems creatively. These problems may be as small as deciding which street to take to school or as significant as choosing whom you should marry. You might say that each time you make a decision, you are using both critical thinking and problem-solving strategies. John Chaffee (1995), author of *The Thinker's Guide to College Success,* wrote the following:

> Becoming an effective problem solver does not merely involve applying a problem-solving method in a mechanical fashion, anymore than becoming a mature critical thinker involves mastering a set of thinking skills. Rather, solving problems, like thinking critically, reflects a total approach to making sense of experience. When we think like problem solvers, we approach the work in a distinctive way. Instead of avoiding difficult problems we have the courage to meet them head-on and the determination to work through them. Instead of acting impulsively or relying exclusively on the advice of others, we are able to make sense of complex problems in an organized way and develop practical solutions and initiatives.

Problem solving requires brainstorming, analyzing, and considering every aspect of an issue. Only by rejecting mediocre solutions can problem solvers strive to uncover more innovative solutions. By implementing six easy steps to problem solving, learners can integrate crucial problem-solving strategies, which will echo far beyond the school years and reverberate during a lifetime of learning.

Steps to Effective Problem Solving

COGNITION refers to thinking processes like reasoning, knowing, and perceiving.

Solving problems is a cognitive process. You will need to use every thinking process possible (reasoning, knowledge, perception, judgment). These processes are the ones that allow you to make sense out of your life and help you find solutions when you think there may not be any available. Understanding the need for problem solving is sometimes easier than knowing how to implement the problem-solving process. The following steps will guide you as you work toward finding solutions to problems or conflicts.

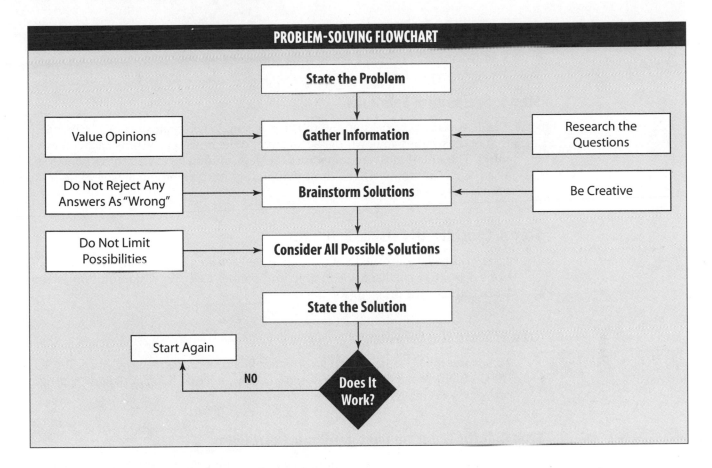

Step 1: State the Problem

State the problem specifically. By stating the problem in verbal or written form, the potential solution becomes clear. As you work through the steps, you might find that your perception about the problem has changed. Consequently, the problem statement may change once the solution to the problem is found.

Write down ideas, thoughts, perceptions, and potential solutions to your problem on 3" × 5" cards or in a notebook. This will help you organize your thoughts. Seeing the problem in a list or written on a card helps to simplify it.

Drawing or diagraming a problem may enable you to understand it better. It is also an enjoyable way to analyze the various aspects of the problem without attacking them directly.

Step 2: Gather Information

It is easy to overlook important details when analyzing factors relating to problems. Breaking down problems into specific areas increases your ability to gather information and understand that potentially more than one problem exists. Make sure that all of your data, research, and information are credible. Be leery of gossip, hearsay, and misinformation when finding solutions.

Gather as much factual information as you can. You probably would not buy a car without first researching potential problems. So why should you solve problems without first researching the issues surrounding the subject?

Talk to everyone about the problem. After speaking to them, consider which advice is best for you. Open your mind to all ideas and think freely about potential solutions. Reiterate the problem: put it in different words. Sometimes saying things differently helps you look at the problem with new understanding. Rethink

REITERATE means to repeat, rephrase, or restate for the purpose of clarification.

the problem, acknowledging old perceptions while creating workable new ones. By relying on your research, education, and knowledge base you will be able to make a more informed decision as you solve the problem.

Step 3: Brainstorm Solutions

Think of every possible solution to the problem. When brainstorming, remember that no answer is bad or wrong. Be creative. Write down everything that comes to mind. The silliest ideas are sometimes the best solutions. When you refuse to look at all of the alternatives, you limit your ability to solve problems. Every item on your list is a potential solution.

Step 4: Consider All Possible Solutions

After you have completed your list, analyze each item, narrowing possible solutions down to a smaller list. Question and ponder every potential solution as you work through the problem-solving steps.

Step 5: State the Solution

This is the time you have been waiting for. It is time to decide how you will solve the problem. What is your final solution? Now, make it happen! Follow through on your decision and solve that problem!

Step 6: If the Solution Does Not Work, Start Over

In most cases, the solution will be great, and you will not even need to question such a well-thought-out decision. However, there are times when the solution does not work. If this happens, go back to Step 1 and work through the problem-solving steps until it *does* work.

The More You Use These Steps, the Easier They Will Be to Apply.

By combining critical thinking and problem-solving strategies, you will become a more efficient thinker. You will be able to assess lectures, readings, movies, and personal relationships more reasonably and effectively. You will find that by using the skills learned in this chapter you will be able to think more logically, productively, and deeply. As the world changes rapidly around you, critical thinking and problem-solving strategies are vital to adapting and surviving. It is through the use of critical thinking skills that you will be more adept in assessing goals, making informed decisions, collecting and understanding data, and understanding the implications and consequences of your behavior.

Failure Is Okay Sometimes

One potential consequence of problem-solving behavior is failure. Failure is not all bad. Sometimes failure brings with it more creative, useful information than success would, the first time around. For instance, the little multicolored Post-it notes used currently in offices were created by mistake. The workers at 3M had a batch of glue that would not work and set it aside as a failure. Later, a 3M employee was singing in his church choir and became frustrated with the little pieces of paper that kept falling out of his hymnal. He went back to the lab and asked if they had glue that would stick and unstick. They pulled out the "failed" glue, and Post-it notes were created. Post-it notes are a shining example of a failure that became both useful and profitable. You, too, can use past failures to bolster future successes.

Brainstorming Solutions to Your Problems

The purpose of this exercise is to provide you with experience in brainstorming solutions to your problems.

It is one thing to read about brainstorming. It is another to know how it feels to brainstorm problems that might seem unresolvable. Choose a problem (academic or personal) and solve it by using the six problem-solving steps.

_____

_____

_____

_____

_____

_____

_____

_____

_____

_____

_____

_____

Step Inside . . . The Internet

Critical thinking is essential when learning, and what better place to learn than the Internet? Multitudes of topics are available at your fingertips. When you want to add to the information presented in readings or lectures, or research a new topic, the Internet can supplement your learning. However, the information presented on the Internet must be viewed while employing every critical learning skill you have studied in this chapter.

The readings in your text are usually researched, written, rewritten, reviewed by other professors and editors, and then written again. The reason you need to use your critical thinking skills when using the Internet is because many of the authors are anonymous. No editors or reviewers have checked the information for accuracy, and the presented information may be more opinion than fact. Another concern is that the authors may have no expertise or experience in the field in which they are writing. Be cautious about accepting information presented on-line; just because it is easily available does not mean that it is valid.

**Be Cautious.
Think
Critically.
Be Informed.**

When accessing information on the Net, be critical and ask questions. Be cautious. Be informed. Know who creates the Web page that you are accessing. Sometimes when you think you are accessing academic information, you are really tapping into a commercial source. Be aware of commercial sites that request payment for information that is free from other sites. Most colleges and universities have Internet sites that allow you access to the state library or university library system. These are valid, free sources that will quickly provide you with the information you need. When referencing a Web page, you will always want to know who the author is, what credentials he or she has, the copyright date, and which institution is responsible for the page. Make sure that there are bibliographical references and that the information you are reading on one page is linked to a main page. If it is linked, identify the main source (Sinclair, 1997).

By carefully researching and evaluating each Internet page you access, you will know that the information you choose for class assignments is authentic and well documented. By asking the appropriate questions and assessing sites for accuracy, you will be assured that the projects you create are academically sound.

Internet Exercise

Ask your librarian or instructor to help you step inside the Internet. Choose a topic that is of interest to you, and use a search engine that you are comfortable with (e.g., Yahoo!, Alta Vista, First Search) to find out more about it. Use the following questions as your guide, and record the information on this page.

1. What is the title of the site you found on the Internet?

2. What is the Web site address?

3. What is the copyright date?

4. Who is the author?

5. What is the author's background?

6. Is the site linked to a main page? If so, to which page is it linked?

7. Do you believe that this Internet site is reliable? Why, or why not?

Role Play Félipe

B reak into groups of four or five, and read aloud the setting and role play. You will need to create the ending of this role play through discussion and collaboration in your group. You may change the dialogue and add new characters. Your role play conclusion should demonstrate that you have reflected on the character's perspective and his circumstances. Act out the role play for the class. After each group has acted out its role play, discuss the questions that follow.

Setting: *Félipe and Joe, two workers at the same company, meet in the employees' break room.*

> *Félipe is thirty-two years old, married, and the father of two children, aged four and seven years. His wife Miriam works part time as a teacher's aide. Félipe has just dropped out of college. He found he could not keep up with work, classes, study, and family. One of the major obstacles was his commuting time to work: one hour on good days and up to two-and-a-half hours in heavy traffic. This left him with little time for his family, even though his family life is very important to him. He has been searching actively for a new job. Three companies have offered him a position.*

> *Joe is forty-seven years old and has been Félipe's friend for ten years. Lately he has noticed how irritable and abrupt Félipe has been with him and other co-workers. Joe is married and has two sons, aged nineteen and twenty-two years. He, too, is very close to his family.*

Joe: [*Calls to Félipe, who has just entered the room*] Hey, Félipe. Join me for a cup of what this place passes off as coffee.

Félipe: [*Comes over*] Thanks. [*Gets a cup of coffee*]

Joe: What's wrong? You look like the boss just handed you a pink slip.

Félipe: I wish he would. It would force me to make a decision.

Joe: What's going on?

Félipe: I've got to find another job.

Joe: Why?

Félipe: The commute is killing me. I never see Miriam and the kids.

Joe: Hey, no job is worth that.

Félipe: That's what I've been thinking.

Joe: I've noticed you've been edgy lately. I thought it was because of going back to school.

Félipe: I had to quit. I just couldn't keep up. There goes my degree and my future.

Joe: Hey, get a grip. Things aren't all that bad when you think them through. Have you started looking for another job?

Félipe: Yeah. Three companies have already made me offers.

Joe: That's great. So, which one are you going with?

Félipe: That's just it. I don't know. Making up my mind is driving me crazy. Miriam made me write out the offers on paper so that I could look them over and decide. [*Hands Joe two sheets of paper*]

Joe: [*Reads*] Morris is giving you $23,000 a year, a pretty good health insurance package, stock options, and seven days of vacation. You figured the commute at about twenty-five minutes from home. [*Reads next sheet*] Franzen is offering $23,500, no health insurance, and five vacation days. The commute is about five minutes.... You said three. Where's the last one?

Félipe: Oh, I didn't write that one down yet. It's at Gaylord's. They're offering $26,000 and an HMO insurance plan, but no vacation for the first year. It's about eighteen minutes from my house. So, what do you think?

Continue the dialogue. Help Félipe go through the decision-making process by using critical thinking and problem-solving strategies.

Questions

1. Develop a set of criteria by which Félipe can measure his options.

2. Explain how priorities affect the decision-making process.

3. Describe your own set of priorities for finding a job at this time in your life.

Review

This review is correlated with the objectives at the start of the chapter. One way to study Chapter 2 is to look at the objectives, write down everything you learned about each one, and then compare your notes to this review.

1. *Critical thinking is a process in which questioning, challenging, dissecting, and problem solving are important tools in active learning.* Critical thinking forces you to question everything. Critical thinkers question, reason, challenge, and solve problems. They do not accept solutions at face value.

2. *Critical thinking is based on finding new solutions to old problems.* Critical thinkers can create a fresh understanding of problems by examining them from the viewpoint of a child.

3. *Learn without bias and openly discuss controversial issues with others.* Learn to anticipate how your actions and perceptions correlate to thinking critically. Try to be open to new or different ideas when involved in discussions with others. Learn to think differently, rediscover the child within you, question and challenge facts, open your mind, discuss issues with others, anticipate negative and positive implications, let your mind wander and be intuitive.

4. *Problem solving is the ability to work out solutions creatively.* Problem solvers integrate critical thinking by rejecting initial, easy solutions in order to uncover innovative solutions.

5. *Problem-solving steps:* The steps to solving problems are (1) state the problem, (2) gather information, (3) brainstorm solutions, (4) consider all possible solutions, (5) state the solution, and (6) if the solution does not work, start again.

6. *Understand that there are times when failure is okay.* Come to terms with failure. Know that failure can bring about useful information and emotional growth.

Setting Goals and Managing Time

CHAPTER 3

OBJECTIVES

By the end of this chapter, you will be able to . . .

1. **List specific ways to turn goals into reality.**

2. **Set goals and plan for their attainment.**

3. **Understand how per-severance, motivation, hard work, and breaking goals into pieces are the foundation of goal attainment.**

4. **Evaluate the way you manage time.**

5. **Create to-do lists and prioritize tasks.**

6. **Create daily, weekly, and monthly time management charts.**

7. **Combat time barriers.**

8. **Stop procrastinating.**

SETTING GOALS AND MANAGING TIME CHECKLIST

The purpose of the following checklist is to help you identify factors that will enable you to manage time effectively.

Check the appropriate answer:

1. Have you created a list of goals that you want to attain? YES _____ NO _____

2. Have you created a plan to carry out your goals? YES _____ NO _____

3. Do you create daily to-do lists? YES _____ NO _____

4. Do you prioritize the tasks that you need to complete daily? YES _____ NO _____

5. Do you like to use a time management chart? YES _____ NO _____

6. Do you create extra time in your schedule to allow for the unexpected? YES _____ NO _____

7. Do you monitor the time you spend watching TV or talking on the phone so that they do not interfere with study time? YES _____ NO _____

8. Do you find ways to reward yourself when you prioritize and manage time effectively? YES _____ NO _____

If you answered yes to all these questions, write which time management techniques work best for you and explain why they are so effective.

_____

_____

_____

_____

If you answered no to any of the questions, read through the chapter and identify ways to improve your time management skills. Write about them.

_____

_____

_____

_____

_____

Exceptional students explore their resources to establish their wants and needs for the present as well as the future. With this foundation they create goals for their overall plan and build objectives to help them achieve each step along the way. They may adopt a new goal or change an existing objective to suit the present situation, but they never lose sight of their target. They are resourceful at adapting to a changing environment and can be compared to a chameleon changing when necessary but supporting its needs all the while.

Bill Draw, student
STATE UNIVERSITY OF NEW YORK, MORRISVILLE, NEW YORK

When you think about your future, who do you want to be in ten years? What are your academic, personal, and financial dreams? How will you make your dreams come true? By acknowledging who you want to be and by positioning dreams within a timely framework, your dreams can become reality. Goals mirror what you want from life, today, tomorrow, and in the distant future. Dreams do not magically come true; they ride on the coattails of goals and are energized by perseverance and desire. For goal attainment to occur, related tasks are intricately woven into daily activities and maintained by motivation. Many people dream about accomplishing amazing goals, but their intentions get lost in the day-to-day actions of turning goals into reality.

This chapter presents ways to set goals, prioritize them, and build them into your daily lifestyle through effective time management. By planning and controlling time, while eliminating time barriers that deter you from reaching goals, you can discover the benefits of taking control of the minutes in your days.

Setting Goals

Turn Goals into Reality

Goals Are Directed Dreams. Their Direction Is up to You.

To get to where you want to be in college or your career, goals and action plans need to be in place. Specific, detailed goals are essential to success. Without goals, it is difficult to target behaviors in a way that will help you be who you want to be in the future. You would not put a boat in a river without a rudder and expect it to reach its destination without mishaps. It will probably hit rocks, sandbars, and river banks. The ride could be bumpy, and the boat could stray into dangerously rough waters. When the boat has a rudder, it can be steered away from rocky areas, prevented from being stalled by sandbars, or capsized by rough waters. Your "rudder" represents your goals. Specific goals will guide you away from the bumps, delays, and rough spots in life. Without goals, direction can be lost.

The heartfelt desire for your goals to become a reality, the visualization of who you want to be, and the effort that creates dreams, are the forces and motivations behind goal creation. When creating dreams, talk to people, and ask advice about

Dreams of achieving goals for athletic or artistic events, college, and life are realized through hard work, action plans, perseverance, and tremendous effort.
© Frank Ward.

your future in college, in your career, or in life. Their feedback can be helpful in making decisions about your goals, but ultimately the goal-making decision rests with you. Set your goals and make them happen.

Set Specific Goals

What is important to you? Setting goals starts with clarifying what you believe will be your most important accomplishments, now and in the future. This all-encompassing task can be simplified by writing down goals. When creating your goal list, include all aspects of your life: academic ambitions, relationships, personal interests, values, career choices, or financial gain. Be sure that each goal is specific, not general. Stay away from words like *good, a lot,* or *great.* A goal that says, "I want to live a good life" or "I want to make a lot of money" is not specific enough for direction and attainment. By defining *a lot* or specifically stating what you would like to attain, the exact measurable direction of your goal becomes clear. For example, "To me a good life means getting married, starting a family, and enjoying my work." "A lot of money means a 60 percent salary increase." Or "A lot of money means not having to struggle to support my family while saving 7 percent of my monthly income."

Create Short-Term and Long-Term Goals

SHORT-TERM GOALS are tasks you would like to accomplish today, in the next few weeks or months, or during the next year.

LONG-TERM GOALS are tasks you would like to accomplish in the years to come.

What are your lifelong goals? What do you want to do with the rest of your life? It is important to create short-term and long-term goals to ensure that you adopt behaviors now that will guarantee the attainment of your goals later. Short-term goals are established with the hope that you can accomplish them soon. Long-term goals are based on your future dreams. By creating a list of short-term and long-term goals it is easier to direct daily actions in ways that goals will become a reality. By categorizing goals into lifelong, ten-year, two-year, this semester, or two-week frameworks, you are providing a blueprint for goal achievement. Copy your goals and place them on your refrigerator or mirror as a constant reminder of your goal-oriented plans.

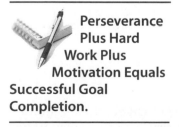

Perseverance Plus Hard Work Plus Motivation Equals Successful Goal Completion.

Perspiration Prompts Progress

When creating goals, find ways to make them happen. In the book *Edison: A Life of Invention,* P. Israel (1998) quotes Edison as saying, "Genius is 1 percent inspiration and 99 percent perspiration." This quote reflects the need to generate actions (perspiration) to create goals. Goals will not progress by simply thinking about them; action generates success.

Create an Action Plan

Actions create goals. Without direction, goals sometimes lose momentum. One way to capture direction is to create an action strategy. An action plan is a written

An **ACTION PLAN** is a written outline of steps that will support the achievement of goals.

strategy that supports your need to achieve short-term and long-term goals. Your plan can be a sentence fragment written on a Post-it note, a to-do list hung on your refrigerator, a notation in your calendar, or an intricate, detailed chart. The design is not as important as your following through with your plan. Action plans serve as reminders to finish specific tasks (daily) in order to reach all goals.

Break Goals into Small Chunks

Goals can be achieved by breaking them into small chunks. It is easier to achieve small goals day-by-day than it is to attack a huge goal at the last minute. Large goals may seem overwhelming. By breaking goals into small segments, they become achievable. For example, if the instructor says on the first day of class, "There are eighty-five terms from the glossary that you will need to know for the fill-in-the-blanks final. Please learn them on your own, as we will not go over them in class," you will need to create an action plan to ensure that when the final comes around, you have learned all eighty-five terms. Your action plan could be to learn seven terms the first week and six terms for each week thereafter (assuming a fourteen-week semester). By writing them in your weekly calendar, you are providing a consistent reminder to finish them within an appropriate time frame. By finals week, all terms could be mastered. This type of action plan creates confidence, alleviates stress, encourages time management, and promotes goal completion.

Pat Yourself on the Back

When you do achieve a goal (small or large), reward yourself for work well done. Rent a movie, spend extra time on a hobby, or acknowledge the good feeling you get when you meet your own expectations. Small reinforcements along the way ensure the pursuit of long-term goal attainment.

Reevaluate Goals to Stay Motivated

The realization of goals is based on the strength of your motivational levels. When motivation is weak and goals seem impossible, what will you do? Reevaluate your goals. Have you made the right choices? When you originally create your goals, set dates for self-evaluation. You may want to change some goals or break them into even smaller parts. You may want to change the time frame for the goal or change the goal totally. For example, after one semester in the computer programming curriculum, you may reevaluate and decide that a business curriculum is better for you.

You may want to seek support from others as you reevaluate your goals. Ask yourself who can remind or reinforce you in ways that will keep you motivated. Sometimes others can prod your desire to be motivated while helping you clarify goals. Admitting that you need help, talking to instructors, college tutors, counselors, advisors, or peers is better than getting discouraged and giving up. Find your support systems, and ask them for help. Do not let goals dissipate because you did not want to ask for support.

Visualize Your Goals

VISUALIZATION entails getting comfortable, closing your eyes, and creating in your mind a detailed picture of yourself achieving a goal.

By visualizing your success, it is more likely to happen. Often, visualization of yourself reaching the goal is a strong motivator that assists in reinvestment in the day-to-day activity needed to make dreams happen. Ask yourself what the end result will be when you attain this goal. By focusing on the end result of the goal, motivation increases.

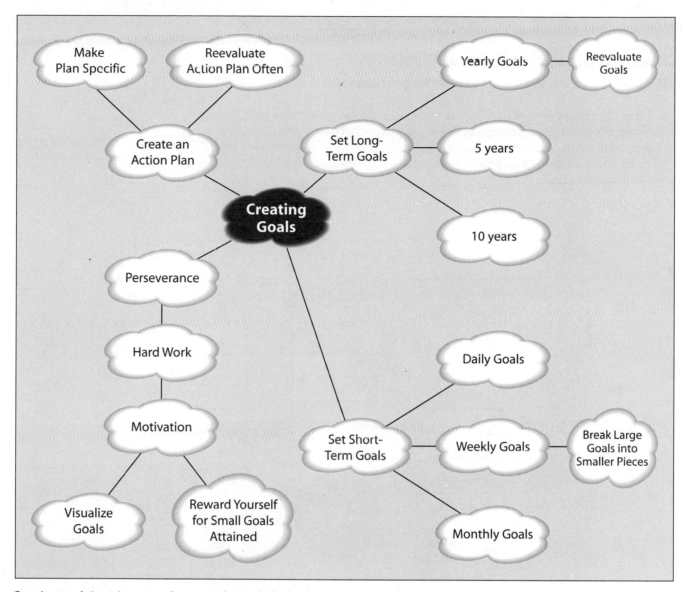

Creating goals is an integrated process that includes many interrelated facts.

QUICK CHECK

Think of a goal. Write it down. Now, close your eyes, relax, and visualize yourself accomplishing it. How did your visualization reinforce your desire to attain your goal?

Visualization entails getting comfortable, closing your eyes, and picturing yourself achieving a specific goal. Make your visualization realistic and specific. If your goal is to graduate with honors, visualize yourself walking across the stage, shaking the hand of the university president, wearing a gold honors rope over your graduation gown. That vivid image becomes a significant part of your motivation when times get tough and motivation is hard to find. Anyone who has played sports knows how important visualization is in realizing success in an athletic event. It is no different when striving to claim your college victories.

Believing in yourself and knowing that you can reach your goal is crucial to goal development. By persevering, goals turn into real-life events. Your dreams and goals can be attained only by making them specific, and by creating a supportive action plan that will help ensure their development. Sometimes you will need to be willing to make sacrifices to accomplish goals. Hard work and detailed planning integrated with effective time management makes goals and dreams come to life as a reality.

Create a Blueprint for Your Goals
The purpose of this exercise is to practice goal setting.

1. Fill in the blanks with realistic goals that can be achieved within a specific time frame of one semester, one year, five years, ten years, twenty years, and your entire life. Make your goals specific, realistic, and achievable. Make sure the goals cover all aspects of your life: financial, academic, personal, career, health, and so on.

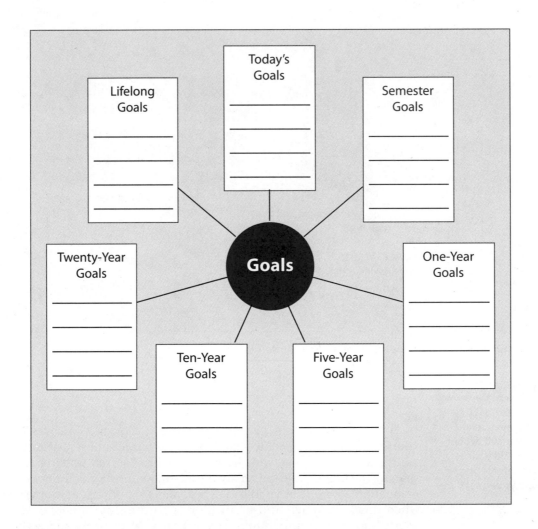

2. Choose three goals from the first part of this exercise:

   a. _____

   b. _____

   c. _____

3. Write about each of the three goals you listed in the second part of this exercise. Why is each goal important to you? How will you achieve each one? What barriers could potentially prevent you from obtaining each goal? What behavioral changes will you need to make to assure the completion of each goal?

_____

_____

_____

_____

_____

_____

_____

_____

_____

_____

_____

_____

_____

_____

_____

_____

_____

_____

_____

_____

_____

_____

_____

_____

Managing Time

Time is a resource that you can control only by using it wisely; you cannot slow it down or speed it up or save it for another day. Time belongs to you; how you use it is your decision. Managing time permits you to do your best in your courses while enabling you to enjoy the free time you do have because you will have earned it and looked forward to it.

When time is managed efficiently, free time exists without guilt. Stress dissipates because projects, papers, and studying are done ahead of time, eliminating the anxiety that is created by procrastination. You know the old adage "Don't put off until tomorrow what you can do today," but you also are familiar with "Easier said than done." Time management conflicts lie between wanting to get things done (intentions) and getting them done (actions).

When you take charge of time, it becomes easier to listen to and focus on lectures or studying because you can concentrate on the tasks at hand rather than worry about whether you have enough time to complete them. The workload and pace in college are usually faster than they were in high school; there may be more activities and distractions that pull you away from your studies. The challenge is to make the most out of every minute by understanding how long it will take to complete each task. One way to do this is to use time estimation.

Time Estimation

One way to conquer time is to estimate how long it will take you to complete each task. You can learn to control time by trying to finish each task within an estimated time frame. Before you start a task, estimate how much time you will need to complete it effectively. Add a few minutes to your time estimates to compensate for the frustrating fact that it often takes longer to complete tasks than you think it will. By estimating time on a task, you learn to control the use of the minutes in your day.

Charles Has 168 Hours to Use This Week. What Will He Do with Them?

	168 hours
Sleep (8 hrs/night)	−56
	112 hours
Eat (2 hrs/day)	−14
	98 hours
Part-time job	−20
	78 hours
Travel time (1.5 hrs/weekday)	−7.5
	70.5 hours
Classes	−15
	55.5 hours
Study time (2 hrs/each class hour)	−30
	25.5 hours
Chores + pay bills	−7
	18.5 hours

Charles has 18.5 hours left per week to use any way he wants.

How Do You Use Your Minutes?

When you have many tasks to complete in a short period of time, do you find that you do not have a clue about how to get everything done? There are 168 hours in the week. After you sleep, eat, attend classes, study, work, travel to and from work and school, and visit with your friends, how many hours do you have left? Charles, a college freshman, completed everything that "must be done" and had 18.5 hours left per week—a little under 3 hours per day—which he could use for leisure activities, time with friends or family, appointments, or "emergencies." By understanding how much time is dedicated to daily required tasks (sleeping, eating, traveling, studying), you will be able to figure out more easily how to manage your time efficiently.

Where Does Your Time Go?

The purpose of this exercise is to figure out how you use your time.

Fill in the time estimation chart. Remember to include time for travel (to and from school or work), friends and family, leisure activities, and appointments.

What Will You Do with 168 Hours This Week?

168

Study group	_____ hrs	Sleep	_____ hrs
Eating	_____ hrs	Work	_____ hrs
Classes	_____ hrs	Exercise	_____ hrs
Study time	_____ hrs	_____	_____ hrs
_____	_____ hrs	_____	_____ hrs
_____	_____ hrs	_____	_____ hrs
_____	_____ hrs	_____	_____ hrs
_____	_____ hrs	_____	_____ hrs

How many hours do you have left? How will you use them?
How can this estimation chart help you manage your time better?

Creating Priorities

PRIORITIZATION is combining tasks and time together in an orderly fashion.

A major step in working within time management guidelines is sorting out priorities. One way to do this is to create a to-do list that includes everything you need to get done within a twenty-four-hour period. After creating the list, find ways to rearrange the list and prioritize tasks so that the most important ones get done first. The stress of accomplishing much in a short period of time lessens when you know what should be done first, second, and third. School, work, and personal tasks can be prioritized. In most cases, it is simpler to put all three categories on one list because you can see the consistency between all of the tasks.

The most commonly used criterion to prioritize goals is the importance of the task. For example, studying for a biology test may take priority over washing your clothes (unless they have not been washed for a few weeks). When creating a to-do list, you might list the biology test as 1 and the laundry as 2. Once you establish the

importance of the task, you will be better prepared to follow through on finishing all of your tasks.

This prioritized list can serve as a reminder of what needs to be accomplished daily. Sometimes, just writing and prioritizing a to-do list will help you remember everything that needs to be done. Other times, the list needs to be detailed and placed in an obvious location so you will not forget. For example, place Post-it notes on the mirror for morning reminders or on the dashboard for traveling reminders. Create to-do lists and experiment with them until you find what works for you. As an example, José's to-do list and his prioritization of one day's tasks are shown on page 45.

By Ruth Flanigan

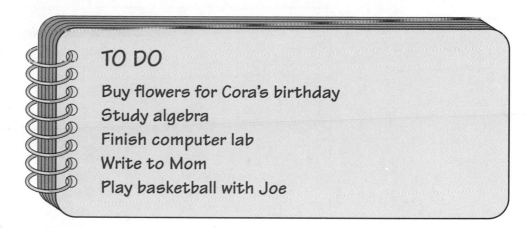

TO DO

Buy flowers for Cora's birthday
Study algebra
Finish computer lab
Write to Mom
Play basketball with Joe

José's to-do list.

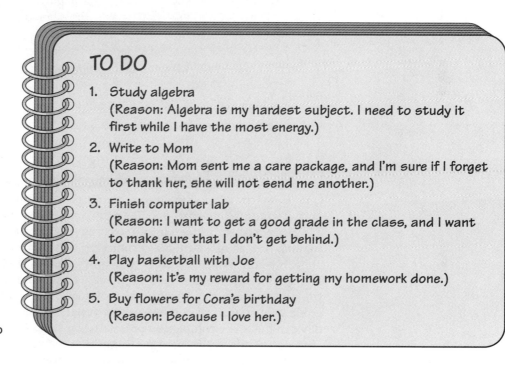

TO DO

1. Study algebra
    (Reason: Algebra is my hardest subject. I need to study it first while I have the most energy.)

2. Write to Mom
    (Reason: Mom sent me a care package, and I'm sure if I forget to thank her, she will not send me another.)

3. Finish computer lab
    (Reason: I want to get a good grade in the class, and I want to make sure that I don't get behind.)

4. Play basketball with Joe
    (Reason: It's my reward for getting my homework done.)

5. Buy flowers for Cora's birthday
    (Reason: Because I love her.)

How José prioritized his to-do list.

Time Management Charts

A **TIME MANAGEMENT CHART** lists what you hope to accomplish in a specific period of time.

A time management chart organizes time. It reminds you of your time commitment so that the day does not end without you meeting your goals. It is a guide that can be used to encourage the completion of tasks and the prevention of time squandering. To-do lists serve as an effective reminder of daily goals. By recording tasks from the to-do list into a chart, your awareness of what needs to be done increases. Sometimes tasks seem so large that you wonder how you will be able to accomplish all of them. By breaking big tasks into smaller ones and listing them within a time framework, you make them more manageable. José took his prioritized to-do list (shown above) and integrated it into a time management chart for one day (shown on page 46); then he typed a time management chart for three days (shown on page 47).

Many people rely on daily planners or calendars to organize their time charts. Weekly projections of time use are important in staying ahead of time management conflicts because they allow you to see the day-to-day listing of tasks while

Monday, January 10

6:00 A.M. – 7:00 A.M.	Get up, shower, breakfast
7:00 A.M. – 8:00 A.M.	Study algebra
8:00 A.M. – 9:00 A.M.	Study algebra
9:00 A.M. – 10:00 A.M.	Work on computer lab at home
10:00 A.M. – 11:00 A.M.	Write to Mom/get ready for school/ put gas in car
11:00 A.M. – 12:00 P.M.	Drive to college/eat lunch
12:00 P.M. – 1:00 P.M.	Class
1:00 P.M. – 2:00 P.M.	Class
2:00 P.M. – 3:00 P.M.	Class
3:00 P.M. – 4:00 P.M.	Visit friends
4:00 P.M. – 5:00 P.M.	Computer lab
5:00 P.M. – 6:00 P.M.	Drive home/buy Cora flowers
6:00 P.M. – 7:00 P.M.	Eat dinner
7:00 P.M. – 8:00 P.M.	Play basketball
8:00 P.M. – 9:00 P.M.	Relax
9:00 P.M. – 10:00 P.M.	Watch TV with Cora

José's time management chart for one day.

providing a seven-day perspective of what is to come. As you prepare your weekly calendar, reflect on your long-term goals and tie them into your daily and weekly activities. This will help you to remember that what you do today and tomorrow makes your lifelong goals become reality.

Time charts work well for some because they provide the needed structure and reminders that make the day comfortable and productive. A time management chart is not intended to create time obsessiveness that prevents daily enjoyment. Its intent is to encourage you to increase organization, complete tasks, and make the most of your day within time boundaries. It is a planner whose design is to guide your time in ways that work for you. Looking at your chart at the end of the day can make the completion of tasks rewarding: You are reminded of all that you have accomplished. If there are things that remain unfinished, place them on the chart for tomorrow. Rather than becoming frustrated by what you did not complete, take stock of the tasks that you finished whether or not they were on your to-do list. There are times in every day that watching a sunset or laughing with friends rejuvenates us. These times cannot be programmed into time charts because their spontaneity is what makes them valuable.

Experiment with the chart and see what works for you. Even if you do not feel you can follow a schedule, it is still important to pay attention to your time use and learn how to respond to time demands without procrastination.

Life's Little Emergencies

Anticipate the Unexpected and Plan for It!

How do you schedule for the unexpected? One of the challenges in conquering time is working within the constraints of unexpected events. Sometimes, life's little emergencies arise when you least expect them. They may prevent or stall the completion of listed tasks. Do not assume, for example, that because you have a free weekend you will be able to finish that last-minute project. Sometimes, when you count on a span of time for task completion, minicrises gobble up your time. For example, you are studying for your earth science test when your dog jumps the fence and runs away. Earth science waits while you run through the neighborhood looking for Duke! It waits even longer as you ride to the neighborhood pound to pick him up. There is lit-

Monday, January 10

8:00 A.M.	Study algebra	1:00 P.M.	Computers 110
9:00 A.M.	Work on computer lab report	2:00 P.M.	Computers 110
10:00 A.M.	Get gas-Write to Mom	3:00 P.M.	Student union/Josh and Kiersten
11:00 A.M.	RELAX	4:00 P.M.	Computer lab/Finish lab report
12:00 P.M.	Computers 110	5:00 P.M.	Buy Cora flowers
Put computer disks in backpack. Make reservations for dinner tomorrow night.		NIGHT:	Play basketball with Joe. Go to Cora's house

Tuesday, January 11

8:00 A.M.		1:00 P.M.	Finish research project
9:00 A.M.	Dentist appointment	2:00 P.M.	Play chess with Leon
10:00 A.M.		3:00 P.M.	
11:00 A.M.	Study group	4:00 P.M.	Algebra 148
12:00 A.M.		5:00 P.M.	Algebra 148
Pack algebra notes for study group and list of questions for advisor in backpack.		NIGHT:	Take Cora to dinner

Wednesday, January 12

8:00 A.M.	English class/Hand in research project	1:00 P.M.	Hand in computer lab report
9:00 A.M.	English class	2:00 P.M.	Computer lab
10:00 A.M.	Writing lab	3:00 P.M.	Computer lab
11:00 A.M.		4:00 P.M.	
12:00 P.M.	Meeting with advisor, Room 212/Academics	5:00 P.M.	Buy poster board for English project
Schedule appointment to take Duke to the vet.		NIGHT:	Pick up Cora at 7:00 P.M. Meet Cora's parents at The Old Inn at 7:30 P.M.

José's time management chart for three days.

tle that you can do about unexpected events. The important thing to remember when scheduling your time is to anticipate that minicrises will definitely happen. Anticipate the unexpected, and plan for it. If no crisis occurs, the worst that could happen would be that you would have extra time—perhaps for a walk with your dog.

Time management is a strategy that can be learned by paying attention to how you spend time. Time management charts are effective when you understand that time is best used when planned. Anticipating change, scheduling extra time for the unexpected, working ahead, and being flexible go a long way in accomplishing tasks.

It is important to schedule fun into your time management chart as a reward for completing academic tasks.
© Chuck Savage / THE STOCK MARKET.

 EXERCISE

Managing Time Through Practice

The purpose of this exercise is to practice listing tasks, prioritizing them, estimating the time needed for each task, and creating a time management chart.

It is suggested that you complete this exercise daily and use the following steps.

1. Record all tasks that need to be completed in the to-do list for that day.

2. Go back and prioritize all tasks, so that you know which task to start first.

3. Estimate the amount of time each task will take.

To-Do List

Date: _____

Task	Estimated Time for Task Completion
_____	_____
_____	_____
_____	_____
_____	_____
_____	_____
_____	_____
_____	_____
_____	_____

TIME MANAGEMENT CHART

Date: _____

6:00 A.M. – 7:00 A.M.	6:00 P.M. – 7:00 P.M.
7:00 A.M. – 8:00 A.M.	7:00 P.M. – 8:00 P.M.
8:00 A.M. – 9:00 A.M.	8:00 P.M. – 9:00 P.M.
9:00 A.M. – 10:00 A.M.	9:00 P.M. – 10:00 P.M.
10:00 A.M. – 11:00 A.M.	10:00 P.M. – 11:00 P.M.
11:00 A.M. – 12:00 P.M.	11:00 P.M. – 12:00 A.M.
12:00 P.M. – 1:00 P.M.	12:00 A.M. – 1:00 A.M.
1:00 P.M. – 2:00 P.M.	1:00 A.M. – 2:00 A.M.
2:00 P.M. – 3:00 P.M.	2:00 A.M. – 3:00 A.M.
3:00 P.M. – 4:00 P.M.	3:00 A.M. – 4:00 A.M.
4:00 P.M. – 5:00 P.M.	4:00 A.M. – 5:00 A.M.
5:00 P.M. – 6:00 P.M.	5:00 A.M. – 6:00 A.M.

4. Enter this information into your time management chart for that day at the appropriate time.

5. Evaluate this time management technique. In what ways does it work for you? In what ways do you need to alter it for your personal use?

   You may want to photocopy the following plan and place it in the front of a three-ring notebook so that you can enter due dates for papers, quizzes, or presentations, important meetings, or goal reminders. This can be used in place of a weekly schedule as a more global look at time management. Some students prefer to create a semester plan so that they can include midterms, finals, and important social functions.

MONTH

Monday	Tuesday	Wednesday	Thursday	Friday	Saturday	Sunday

QUICK CHECK

List three time barriers that keep you from finishing tasks.

1. ....
....
2. ....
....
3. ....
....

POTENTIAL TIME BARRIERS (AND SOLUTIONS)	
Forgetting tasks that need to be done	(Write them down.)
Allowing yourself to be easily distracted	(Focus on task.)
Allowing others to dominate your time	(Just say no.)
Being disorganized	(Organize!)
Daydreaming	(Let the thought go, and refocus.)
Telephone, e-mail, video games, TV, Net surfing	(Use as rewards after tasks are finished.)

Combat Time Barriers

TIME BARRIERS are events that prevent you from finishing tasks.

Time barriers are events that prevent you from finishing tasks that you know need to be completed. Be aware of them. Sometimes you will need to use them to clear your mind before you study, use them as a reward for studying, or to do "just because." Know which ones are your vice and enjoy them, but do not let them be a barrier to reaching your goals.

Stop Procrastinating

PROCRASTINATION is delaying completion of tasks.

Procrastination refers to putting things off to the last minute and then becoming frustrated because (1) you will not be able to finish the task by the deadline, (2) you will finish the task by the deadline but the quality will be lacking, or (3) you begin to question whether you have the skills and ability necessary to finish the task. The following excerpt from a student's diary points to many issues that correlate to procrastination:

> I needed this new job, but now it is taking up too much of my time. I have always received A's or B's in my classes; what is wrong with me, why can I not get serious about math? I was supposed to study last night, but instead Jan called and asked me to go out with her for pizza. I felt that I should go, because she had just broken up with her boyfriend. She needed a friend to listen to her. Once we got to the pizza place a bunch of our friends were there, and we all decided to go out dancing. I got home after midnight and started studying. I fell asleep on my books and missed my 7:00 A.M. math quiz. I do not know what I was thinking. Why did I do this?

The following questions should be considered when eliminating procrastination.

Why Don't You Say No?   The student, whose diary entry you just read, may have been caught up in her desire to help her friend, feeling that friendship was more important than studying. She may not have known how to say, "No, I have to study tonight, how about tomorrow night?" By making the choice to be there for her friend, she gave up her own goals (studying math for two hours and attending every class). Sometimes procrastination is caused by being torn between several things that you want to do. The key is in prioritizing which ones you will do now and which ones can wait. Before you say yes to others, think about your response and the effect it will have on you. It may be hard to say no to people you care about, but if you explain the situation, they will usually respect your priorities. If you decide to say yes, then you have chosen to deal with the ramifications of not getting things done that are important to you (e.g., studying for a quiz).

From What Are You Protecting Yourself?

Dr. Sandra Davis (1997), an industrial psychologist, states in *How to Overcome Procrastination:*

> No behavior is continued unless it has a payoff. While you might like to believe that the misery you feel as a result of procrastinating could not possibly be rewarding, in fact, it is. Somewhere, somehow, it must net you something. Procrastination is another word for protectionism. In almost all cases, by procrastinating we protect ourselves from something else that feels far more difficult to face.

In the case of the student quoted earlier, she may have been protecting herself from her fear that she lacked the ability to learn new math concepts. It is easier to rationalize that you should comfort a friend than it is to confront the underlying fear that not understanding mathematical concepts today might mean failure tomorrow. By delaying studying and by not taking the quiz, she did not have to confront her frustration about not understanding math. She was protecting herself from fear of failure.

Do You Really Need to Be That Perfect?

You may find that in your desire to achieve the best grades, be the best student, and do your best in college, you are placing more stress on yourself than is necessary. The perception that you must always be the best can cause anxiety. Anxiety can increase your performance, or it may prevent you from finishing tasks that would normally lead toward success. Frustration may be experienced because it becomes harder to become the replica of perfection that exists in your perception of who you want to be. In the process of searching for perfection, anxiety sometimes interferes with homework completion and class attendance. Consequently, in the effort to achieve quality in *all* tasks completed, the accomplishment of goals can become elusive. The ultimate end to this circle of perfectionism is that some students begin to procrastinate and eventually choose to do nothing. Monitor your perceptions, and be sure that they do not feed into self-defeating procrastinating behavior (Davis, 1997).

Why Are You Procrastinating?

Complete the Quick Check on this page. Whatever the first step is, do it right away. By simply starting the task, it may be easier to follow it to completion. Just by looking at it, thinking about it, and preparing to do it, your interest level and energy level might change. When the task is in front of you, it becomes a gentle reminder of how important it really is. As you sit there, you may find that you even enjoy completing the task. Sitting in front of the TV, thinking you should get busy, does not have the same motivational effect.

Sometimes the thoughts surrounding procrastination are so strong that they prevent you from even beginning. By starting the project immediately, you can win the battle of doing nothing versus getting going.

Are Your Expectations Realistic?

Make sure that the goals you create are realistic. When goals are too demanding, they feed into procrastination. If, for example, the instructor assigns a twenty-page research project and you enter it on your time management chart as being done within two weeks, you are setting yourself up for procrastination. Few instructors would allow only two weeks for

---

QUICK CHECK

Is there a task you are having trouble completing? List three steps that you can follow to stop procrastinating.

1. ....

....

....

2. ....

....

....

3. ....

....

....

a project like this. Break it down into smaller pieces, and change your deadline to four weeks.

What Beckons After This Is Over?   Focus on the reasons and rewards for finishing a task. Visualize what you could be doing if you were not doing this—that visualization might encourage you to hurry up and get it done. Think what it would be like to go to a movie without worrying about when you will be able to finish a specific task. By finishing the task and using the movie as a reward, you will feel less stressed. Seek to find reasons to finish tasks, and take moments to enjoy task completion.

Procrastination is not unusual, but it is important to find ways to stop it before it stops you from achieving goals. You can stop procrastination by understanding why you let it happen and then finding ways to prevent it.

By knowing what your goals are, setting them within a timed framework, and ensuring their achievement through the use of to-do lists, time management charts, and time estimation, your dreams will become reality.

Step Inside . . . An Interview

What better way to learn about time management than from those who currently manage time wisely? Take this opportunity to interview someone who you believe is an excellent manager of time. It could be your professor, a dean, a teaching assistant, or an executive in a company. Use the following questions and add some of your own to learn as much as you can about time management.

1. Why is time management important to you?

    _____

    _____

2. What is the most effective time management technique that you use currently?

    _____

    _____

3. What do you find to be the most difficult part of managing time?

    _____

    _____

4. What advice would you provide to college freshmen about effective time management?

    _____

    _____

5. What part does time management play in your current work?

_____

_____

After you have finished the interview, write a summary of what you have learned.

_____

_____

_____

Internet Exercise

Find a Web site that discusses goal setting and time management. Cite the addresses and authors, and present a list of five concepts that are new to you.

Addresses:

_____

Authors:

_____

_____

Titles:

_____

_____

Concepts:

1. _____

2. _____

3. _____

4. _____

5. _____

Role Play Maria

Break into groups of four or five, and read aloud the setting and role play. You will need to create the ending of this role play through discussion and collaboration in your group. You may change the dialogue and add new characters. Your role play conclusion should demonstrate that you have reflected on the character's perspective and her circumstances. Then, act the role play out for the class, and answer the questions.

Setting: *Maria and her mother, Helen, are talking on the phone.*

Maria is a single mother with two children, age nine and eleven years. For the past two years, she has been working at a convenience mart. She knows that this is a dead-end job and will not pay enough for her to save for her children's future education. Maria has enrolled for two night courses at a community college. She works from 5:00 A.M. to 2:00 P.M. Then she runs errands before picking up her children from school. Both of her children are involved in after-school activities. She drives them to their practices and meetings, cooks dinner, and then goes to her classes. She feels guilty about leaving them alone but cannot afford a sitter. When she comes home from school, she tries to study. Many times she falls asleep over her books.

Helen is Maria's mother. She lives two hundred miles away. Helen was always at home for her children. She was very active in their school activities, helped them with their homework, and was a good homemaker. There was always a good meal for dinner and home-baked treats after school.

Helen: Hi, honey. How are you and the kids?

Maria: Well, right now, Sarah is fighting with Becky over a CD.

Helen: Don't let it upset you. You and your sister always fought.

Maria: It just drives me crazy when they get after each other. I start screaming at them.

Helen: You have to learn to tune out some of those sibling battles.

Maria: I know, Mom.

Helen: I called to tell you about Aunt Carrie.

Maria: Mom, I really don't have time to talk now. I have to drive Becky to her soccer game, and then I have to pick up some eggs and butter to bake some cookies. I will call you later tonight, after my class.

Helen: No. You need your rest. I wish I lived closer to help you, Maria. I will give you a call tomorrow. We need to talk. Love you!

Continue the dialogue. It is the next day. Incorporate advice that you feel Maria's mother will give her to help her manage her time more effectively.

Questions

1. How does Maria view the mother role?

2. What adjustments must she make to this image in order for her to succeed in school?

3. Why is Maria feeling overwhelmed by all that she is doing?

4. Explain how role expectations affect time management behaviors.

Review

This review is correlated with the objectives at the start of the chapter. One way to study Chapter 3 is to look at the objectives, write down everything you learned about each one, and then compare your notes to this review.

1. *Turn goals into reality.* Goals are directed dreams. For goals to become a reality, create a plan, talk to other people, and work toward the achievement of goals.

2. *Acknowledge goals and plan for their attainment.* Clarify the goals that are important now and in the future. Create a plan that will ensure that these dreams become reality. Make sure that the goals are specific, staying away from general words like *great, good,* or *a lot.* Creating goals provides direction; however, no goal can be achieved without purposeful action. Categorize your goals into time constraints by using the parameters of lifelong, ten-year, two-year, this semester, and two-week frameworks.

3. *Perseverance, motivation, hard work, and breaking goals into pieces are the foundation of goal attainment.* To attain goals, success is based on not giving up; it is based on creating actions that will support goals and hard work.

4. *Evaluate the way you manage time.* You can do this by estimating how long it will take you to complete tasks and by creating time management charts with which you practice time management until you become comfortable and understand how you manage time.

5. *Create to-do lists and prioritize tasks.* Creation of to-do lists serves as a daily reminder of what needs to be done to achieve goals. It is a daily list that can be prioritized, with the most important task receiving a number 1.

6. *Create time management charts.* Take your to-do list and integrate it into a time chart that you purchase or create. Just by recording tasks on a chart, your awareness of what needs to be accomplished daily increases. The time management chart reminds you of your time commitments, so that the day does not end without meeting daily goals.

7. *Combat time barriers.* Time barriers are events that prevent you from finishing tasks. Time barriers can be forgetting tasks that need to be completed, allowing yourself to be easily distracted, allowing others to dominate your time, talking on the phone, being disorganized, daydreaming, or overusing video games, TV, or the Internet.

8. *Stop procrastinating.* Procrastination refers to putting things off to the last minute. Stop procrastinating by saying no, understanding your fear of failure, examining your need to be perfect, analyzing why you are procrastinating, and evaluating the reality of your expectations.

Study Strategies

CHAPTER 4

OBJECTIVES

By the end of this chapter, you will be able to . . .

1. Improve your reading study strategies with PQ4R.

2. Master basic study skills.

3. Improve your study environment.

4. Develop more effective ways to learn while in the classroom.

5. Acquire new ways to study math.

6. Study science more effectively.

7. Become more knowledgeable in using a computer as an aid to studying.

8. Understand the curve of forgetting and how it affects learning.

9. Use memory triggers such as coding, acronyms, acrostics, and association.

STUDY STRATEGIES CHECKLIST

The purpose of the following checklist is to help you diagnose the effectiveness of your study strategies.

Check the appropriate answer:

1. Do you always study in the same area?　　YES _____　NO _____

2. Do you set up your study area before you begin with paper, pencils, erasers, etc.?　　YES _____　NO _____

3. Do you preview your materials before you begin?　　YES _____　NO _____

4. Do you ask yourself questions as you study?　　YES _____　NO _____

5. Have you found satisfactory ways to stay focused as you study?　　YES _____　NO _____

6. When you read, do you visualize pictures, words, and ideas associated with your reading?　　YES _____　NO _____

7. Do you recite terms out loud as you study?　　YES _____　NO _____

8. Do you review notes within twenty-four hours of taking them?　　YES _____　NO _____

9. Do you reflect on lessons learned when you have finished studying?　　YES _____　NO _____

10. Do you study your most difficult subjects first?　　YES _____　NO _____

If you are using effective study strategies, your answer to most of these questions will be yes. If you said yes to most or all of them, write the reasons for your success.

_____

_____

If you said no to several questions, record specifically what you need to learn from this chapter to improve your study skills. Pick a study strategy that you would like to try, and write about its limitations and advantages.

_____

_____

If a [study skill] suggestion doesn't quite feel right or work, I revise it. For instance, in Spanish class, I found it very helpful to recite and repeat when I studied. I would then make flashcards and carry them around with me, quizzing myself whenever I got a free minute. Those two techniques helped me do well in Spanish class, so I decided to try them with other classes, and lo and behold, they worked for those classes as well. The trick was tailoring slightly to fit different courses and finding others that worked as well.

Tonya R. Stratton, student
MADISON AREA TECHNICAL COLLEGE, MADISON, WISCONSIN

If you have ever explained the plot of a movie, described a recently read book to a friend, or prepared for an upcoming exam, you have participated in the learning process. The acquisition of knowledge—an integral part of the learning process—is achieved primarily through study. Through the mastery of study skills you can begin to control the future course of your education, career, and life.

Study skills mastery is not simply memorization. It is understanding, comprehending, questioning, and learning. Learned information is stored in long-term memory, ready for retrieval when necessary. Your study strategies should allow you to remember vital information and retrieve it in the future.

Studying means taking responsibility for the acquisition of knowledge. Making the most of your study time, focusing as you study, and accepting the responsibility to learn make college victories achievable.

When working through this chapter, choose and practice the study techniques you think will make a difference in your current study efforts. This chapter will strengthen your current study habits whether you are reading, attending lectures,

Choose a study area that is compatible with your learning style.
© Jon Feingersh/THE STOCK MARKET.

or participating in lab. With the application of each study strategy, your confidence will increase, and you will begin to study more wisely (not necessarily harder) and learn more.

Improve Your Reading Study Strategies with PQ4R

PQ4R is an efficient study technique that was pioneered by Francis P. Robinson (1970) in his work *Effective Study*. It requires you to focus, get involved, and learn. If you are a student who finds himself or herself staring blankly at a reading assignment without comprehension, you can use PQ4R as a way to get started and to maintain interest in reading assignments.

▶ Preview

▶ Question

▶ Read

▶ Reflect

▶ Recite

▶ Review

PQ4R is effective because it provides structure to the study process. When you begin to use PQ4R, you may feel that it takes too much time. Be patient, keep working, and you will begin to experience its benefits. You may even find that some parts of it work better for you than others. For example, the previewing could be helpful, but if you are a visual learner, recitation may not be as informative. Adapt PQ4R according to your learning style.

Let us take a closer look to see how PQ4R can be used to record and remember what you have gleaned from textbooks, notes, and readings.

P—Preview

Previewing is a quick way to give yourself a general idea of what the assignment is about. It paves the way for you to gain a concrete overview of information before listening to lectures or reading more comprehensively. Previewing can help you attack information that may seem overwhelming before you begin. It provides you with the fundamentals upon which you can build more detailed knowledge.

To preview, scan each chapter page by page quickly, extracting the essentials while acquiring an initial familiarity with the information. Skim the table of contents and all headings, charts, graphs, definitions, chapter summaries, vocabulary lists, italic or bold words, and learning objectives. Sometimes it helps to read the summary first, to get a general feeling for the chapter, and then to go back and preview. Reading the first and last sentences of each paragraph can also provide the main ideas under each heading. If you estimate that the reading assignment will take an hour, preview for approximately five minutes. (Allow a little more time for material that is especially complex.)

As you preview, ask yourself how this new information relates to your education and your career. Look for items with which you are already familiar and then build upon your knowledge. Examine concepts or ideas that interest you or examine new approaches to old ideas.

Q—Question

While reading, write questions in the margins of the text or on your note paper. One way to do this is to turn headings and subheadings into questions. For example, if a heading in a psychology text reads, "Psychoanalysis: Sigmund Freud," you

QUICK CHECK

Choose a chapter that you want to preview. Next, mark the segments as you complete the previewing process.

Table of Contents	_____
Chapter Summary	_____
Vocabulary Lists	_____
Learning Objectives	_____
Headings	_____
Subheadings	_____
Graphs	_____
Charts	_____
Definitions	_____
Words in Bold	_____
Words in Italics	_____

could ask the question: How does Sigmund Freud relate to psychoanalysis? As you read the assignment, answer the question.

Active questioning correlates to active learning. Asking yourself questions as you read forces you to focus on and understand the information you are reading. If you do not ask questions, you may find that your eyes see words your mind never registers. Thoughtful questions indicate that you are reading, digesting, and integrating the written word. Questioning causes you to be more interested and less distracted.

R—Read

QUICK CHECK

Which reading time pattern works best for you?

....

....

....

....

You have previewed and created questions; now it is time to read. Read actively! One goal in your reading might be to answer all of the questions you have created. Pay attention to the words and associate what you are reading with the concepts you already know. Visualize any ideas, pictures, words, or theory that will help you to recall the material. Change the speed at which you are reading based on the difficulty of the material and your understanding of it. You will need to slow down for more difficult materials and pick up speed when you are familiar with the subject. Pause occasionally during your reading time to ask yourself what you have just read. Some reading assignments, because of their complexity, may dictate that you read the chapter more than once.

Time your reading sessions to your needs. It may work to read for thirty to forty-five minutes and then take a ten-minute break as a reward for your effort. Or you may be more comfortable reading in two- or three-hour sessions. Everyone has different concentration rates, so experiment and find the time pattern that works best for you.

Also, try reading at the time of day you focus best. If you can control your schedule, experiment with early morning, lunch-time, or after-dinner sessions. The ones that work best are the ones that you should use routinely.

R—Reflect

Reflection is an integral part of learning that allows you to ponder, contemplate, and rethink what you already know while stretching your mind to integrate new information. After reading a segment of text, put your book down and think about the reading. Allow yourself to be open to any thoughts that come to mind. There can be no time limit or time expectation for reflection, as it depends on the simplicity, complexity, or emotionality of the materials that you are reading.

Reflection solidifies new concepts in your memory through reinforcement. It allows you to look at issues with a new perspective, too. Only through reflecting on reading material can you master it.

R—Recite

Have you ever read an entire page and not remembered one word? The technique of recitation can solve this problem. Rehearsing important points out loud allows you to remember them more easily. Why? Because reciting keeps data in your short-term memory long enough for it to solidify and enter your long-term memory.

Reciting also allows you to use more than one of your senses while studying. Hearing the words through recitation triggers memory, as do sight and touch. That is why writing about your reading, speaking aloud, and following a graph line with your finger as you recite reinforces learning.

How do you use recitation when you study? Read aloud! Read a paragraph, cover the material you have read with your hand, and then recite the main points that you have learned. Another way is to recite terms, concepts, theories, and new information over and over verbally. The experience of hearing your own words is powerful.

Through recitation you will also challenge yourself to know what words say and mean. Hearing the words forces you to stop and examine them for further meaning: What did I just read? What did it mean? This immediate feedback sharpens your focus, increasing understanding and confidence.

Recitation is also practiced in study groups. Teaching the lesson to other group members and asking or answering questions augment your own learning.

R—Review

Cultivate the reviewing habit. Consistent review of recent readings or new notes reinforces learning, especially when done within twenty-four hours. Daily reviewing, even for fifteen minutes per class, eliminates the need for cramming. It is a simple formula: the more you review, the more you remember.

As you conduct your daily review, skip material that you already know; concentrate on concepts that are difficult, confusing, or difficult to remember. If a concept is not clear, look it up, ask your professor or study group members, or review it until it is understandable.

There are many additional tips that will strengthen your study skills. As you read about them, decide which ones you would like to experiment with. But first try out the PQ4R exercise on pages 62 and 63 to reinforce what you have just learned.

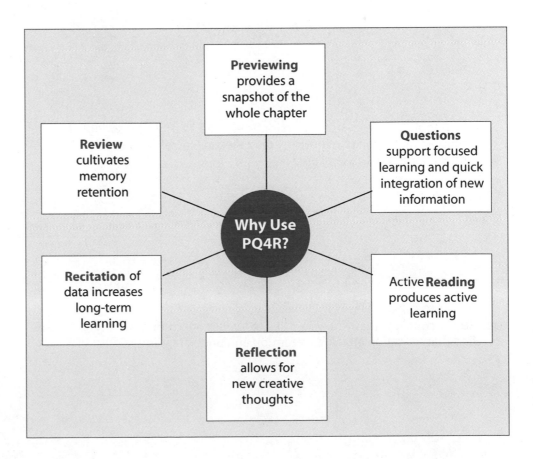

 EXERCISE

Practice PQ4R

The purpose of this exercise is to practice PQ4R using a current reading assignment.

1. Choose a chapter that has been assigned in one of your classes. Use the PQ4R method as you begin the reading assignment.

   a. **Preview** a chapter. List the main concepts that you just learned.

   _____

   _____

   _____

   _____

   b. Write down **questions** you have from the reading assignment and then answer them. (The answers could come from the text, your instructor, or your study group.)

   _____

   _____

   _____

   _____

   c. List new concepts that you learned from **reading.**

   _____

   _____

   _____

   _____

   d. Pick a topic that lends itself to **reflection.** Write (without censoring) any thoughts that come to mind. How did reflection increase your understanding of this concept?

   _____

   _____

   _____

   _____

   e. **Recite** concepts that you would like to learn more comprehensively. Do you find that recitation increases retention and understanding?

   _____

   _____

   _____

   _____

f. **Review.** Describe reviewing techniques that work best for you. Be specific in your description. ("I like to walk around my room, reciting out loud concepts that confuse me.")

_____

_____

_____

_____

2. Which part of PQ4R worked best for you? Which part is least effective? Provide specific examples to support your answer.

_____

_____

_____

_____

_____

3. Which part of PQ4R best matches your learning style? How can you use the information that you learned from this exercise to help you become a more effective learner?

_____

_____

_____

_____

_____

Study Tips

The following helpful hints can assist you in creating the best possible study environment and study habits. The hints are categorized as follows: Master Basic Study Strategies, Control Your Study Environment, Prepare for the Classroom, Find New Ways to Study Math, Study Science More Effectively, and Use a Computer to Support All Study Techniques.

Master Basic Study Strategies

Search for Meaning. Information will not be stored in long-term memory unless you believe it is meaningful. Find ways to create meaning in your assignments. Make sure you know what the information means and how it is relevant to you, and your effort will be rewarded by memory.

Create Interest in Your Subjects. Being interested will enhance your motivation to learn. The more you like what you study, the easier it is to remember. Who wants to remember boring, irrelevant facts? Change your perception and make it interesting.

Learn General Concepts First.   Start with major ideas and concepts. Then break them down into smaller pieces to understand them better.

Manage Your Study Time Wisely.   Make wise decisions about your use of time. Pull out your time management chart, term calendar, or to-do list to keep you on track. Do not procrastinate. Start working on projects and assignments as soon as they are assigned. Thinking "I will do it tomorrow" only creates stress. Set some interim deadlines to keep yourself on schedule.

Schedule Two Hours of Studying Time for Every Class Hour.   This is a formula that you can use to estimate study time weekly. You may find that it works for most classes, or you may find that some classes will take more time and others less. This formula may also change based on the number of tasks that need to be completed and the deadlines attached to each task. Use your priorities as a guide to compute exactly how much time you will need to study each subject.

Study the Hardest Subject First.   Finish the most difficult tasks first. You will have more energy at the start of your study session to tackle tough concepts. Fight the desire to procrastinate. Studying the difficult subject first relieves stress; it also makes the easier subjects seem like a reward for working so hard in the first place.

Overlearn.   You might find yourself studying enough to pass the test. Do you just want to pass the test? Or do you want to learn the information enough to do more than pass the test? You need to permanently remember and understand information in order to do well in advanced classes and learn the skills essential for your career. "Just passing" may not provide you with those skills.

    Instead of memorizing information so that you can regurgitate it later on a test, overlearn for permanent memory storage and retrieval. By asking questions, examining, evaluating, reflecting, and repeatedly relearning information, you can retain more details for tests, for later courses, and for your career.

Know When to Ask for Help.   Tutoring is available on your campus; all you have to do is find it. If you feel that you are falling behind in your studies, ask for help now. Most classes build upon the information already presented. Therefore it is important to seek help before you become lost in the material and fear failure.

Create Effective Study Sessions.   Figure out the amount of study time that works for you. You might study best with fifty-minute study sessions and ten-minute breaks. Or you might learn best by studying for two hours with thirty-minute breaks. You probably do not want to study five or six hours without a break, unless you become so focused on the writing of a paper or so interested in a reading assignment that you could not quit if you wanted to. Experiment with different time spans until you find one that works best for you. No matter what the length of your study session, the more often you study and review, the more you will learn.

Narrow Down Information.   It is frustrating to look at a chapter assignment and feel there is no way you could learn everything. The following suggestions will help you narrow down your reading assignments:

▶   Obvious but important: eliminate anything the instructor said should not be studied.

▶   After previewing the chapter, go back and correlate your lecture notes to the text. Place a star or check next to any information that was emphasized in class, prioritizing the mass of information. You now know those are the areas that you should study first. Then go back and sift through other tidbits of information that would be useful to know.

▶ Try to write down all important concepts on one piece of 8″ × 11″ paper. If you have prioritized accurately, you now can narrow your focus again.

▶ Ask study group members what they feel should be studied and what should be eliminated. Check your assumptions for accuracy, and confirm with your instructor if in doubt.

Be a Kinesthetic Learner (No Head Propping).

Learn by doing! If you passively sit in your chair, propping up your head with your hand, do you think you are really learning? When you study, you need to be energetic and burn calories. That does not usually happen with head propping.

Instead, look for active ways to learn and study. Walk or stand as you read; sing out the words. Throw your note cards on the floor. Stand by each one and see what you can remember about the topic before you pick it up.

Write a term on the front of a Post-it note and a definition on the back: then stick each note to a wall. Walk to the wall, look at the term, and state the definition. Look at the back of the note. Was your answer correct? If you had the right answer, take the note off the wall. If your answer was wrong, leave it on the wall to review later. This process is rewarding because you can immediately see what you have learned and how much is left to master.

Review Your Notes Immediately After Class.

Review your notes while the ideas are still fresh in your mind. It is easier to transcribe words that are difficult to read or fill in fragmented sentences or incomplete thoughts shortly after the lecture. You may not remember this information three or four days from now. Going over your notes after the lecture helps increase memory retention.

Reviewing notes during breaks between classes is an excellent use of time. Find time to review notes again quickly before class begins. This provides continuity as you listen to the new lecture, and it increases retention.

Study When You Are Energetic.

Monitor your energy level. Identify the time of the day when you have the most energy and use it wisely. If you notice that it is easier to concentrate in the morning than at night, you have targeted the best time for you to study. If work schedules or family obligations interfere with your ability to study during your peak times, study as close to the targeted time as possible.

Stay Focused.

Boredom, problems, and daydreaming can all interfere with studying. Find ways to keep yourself focused. Every time your mind wanders, capture your attention and bring it back. Become involved actively in your notes or text instead of focusing passively on your boredom or your personal problems.

If problems divert your attention, write about them. Sometimes jotting down quick notes or reminders on a separate sheet of paper will relieve the anxiety that problems cause, allowing you to quickly refocus on your studies.

If you find that your mind wanders when you start to study, do not despair; it is a common problem. Keep trying; it may take ten or fifteen minutes to get into the study routine.

When you really cannot focus, do study-related tasks. Preview the chapter, rewrite your notes, type key words or definitions on the computer. Actively pursuing related tasks will help you jump into studying quickly.

Visualize Your Lessons.

The more you can create mental pictures of information to be learned, the more memorable the data will be. Draw or visualize the lesson. If you can see it, you are more likely to remember it.

QUICK CHECK

List three study tips that work best for you that are not listed in this chapter.

1. _____

_____

_____

2. _____

_____

_____

3. _____

_____

Every time I sat down to study, I went somewhere that was quiet and well lit. I also made sure that all my friends knew that I was studying and that I didn't want to be bothered. I even unplugged my phone. I made myself study for the time allotted, stopping every fifty minutes to take a ten-minute break. I wasn't so rushed. Soon, it became easier to follow my schedule, and I began to look forward to the quiet time studying would bring me.

Kristian Reese, student
THIEL COLLEGE, GREENVILLE, PENNSYLVANIA

Control Your Study Environment

Always Study in the Same Area.   Studying in the same place all the time improves your concentration. You will not need to constantly adjust to a new study environment, and the inevitable distractions around your study area will be ones that you are used to, so you can deal with them swiftly or even ignore them. If you find that you tire or your attention wanders, walk away from your study area. That way your mind will associate your study area with focused study only.

Experiment with various study locations. Find out whether your desk, the floor, or a library corner works best for you. Avoid studying in bed; falling asleep will not help you in your learning endeavor, and associating active learning with your bed may disrupt your sleeping habits.

Choose Your Study Area Carefully.   Your study environment should be one without distractions. The general rule is no TV, no music, no loud roommates, no ringing phones, and no screaming children. However, the best study environment is a personal choice. You may be able to study only with music on or with your children around you. Experiment. Do not have any qualms, however, about unplugging the phone (or turning on your answering machine), creating mutual study time with your roommates, asking not to be disturbed (hang a sign that says, "Do Not Disturb" or simply say, "I do like you, but I need to study now!"), or creating child-free daily study times.

Choose a Well-Lit Study Area.   When you study in an area that has poor lighting, you may experience eye strain, muscle tension, and irritability. The lack of light may cause you physical discomfort and stress. You want focused concentration when you study, and improper lighting is a distraction and a hazard.

Have Supplies Available Before You Begin.   Do not let your excuse for not studying be that you need a drink, potato chips, pencils, a dictionary, tape, a calculator, disks, or note cards. It is all too easy to waste twenty minutes running back and forth acquiring supplies. Set up your study area before you start studying.

The best study environment is a personal choice. You may be able to study *only* with music on or with your children around you.
© Tony Freeman/PHOTO EDIT.

When you run out of supplies, write them on a shopping list and purchase them ahead of time for your next study session. Do not interrupt your study to go out for things at the last minute.

Prepare for the Classroom

Read Before You Enter the Classroom.   Learning starts before the lecture begins. Be sure you have completed the homework and have read the assignment before entering the classroom. Difficult or uninspiring lectures are easier to understand and remember if you know what the instructor is talking about before he or she begins. The assimilation of data takes less effort when you are prepared. Accept responsibility for preparing yourself.

Monitor Your Attention Level.   How attentive are you? Learn to focus on the lecture. Control your daydreams and your attention level. When daydreams or problems pull your focus away, bring yourself back and refocus on classroom activities.

Be There.   Do not miss class. Attendance correlates to effective learning and the achievement of high grades. It is hard to know what to study if you are not in class to find out. If you have an emergency and cannot attend, make sure you borrow notes from a reliable friend and record them accurately. If you know ahead of time that you will be absent, ask your instructor what work you will miss and prepare it for next time.

Keep a Positive Attitude.   A positive attitude keeps you open to new ideas and alters old perceptions. Coming into class with the attitude "I will learn something today" correlates directly to the amount of energy you will put into learning and how much you will get out of it.

Listen and Participate in Class.   Listening and participating are both integral parts of the learning process in the classroom. It is difficult to gather accurate notes if you are not listening effectively. It is advantageous to participate in class. Active participation makes remembering easier. (Some instructors encourage discussion and debates; others will not tolerate them. Know the instructor's rules.)

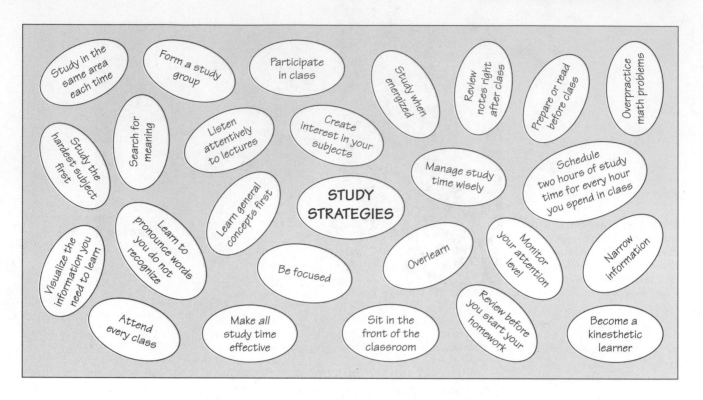

Study in the same area each time

Form a study group

Participate in class

Study when energized

Review notes right after class

Prepare or read before class

Overpractice math problems

Study the hardest subject first

Search for meaning

Listen attentively to lectures

Create interest in your subjects

Manage study time wisely

Schedule two hours of study time for every hour you spend in class

Learn general concepts first

STUDY STRATEGIES

Visualize the information you need to learn

Learn to pronounce words you do not recognize

Be focused

Overlearn

Monitor your attention level

Narrow information

Attend every class

Make all study time effective

Sit in the front of the classroom

Review before you start your homework

Become a kinesthetic learner

Sit in the Front of the Classroom.   It is hard to fall asleep in the front row. If you are in the back, there are too many distractions and too much distance between you and the instructor. Choose the front whenever possible.

Make Sure Friends Are a Help, Not a Hindrance.   If your friends keep you from being focused on the lecture, let them know that their behavior is not acceptable to you. If they refuse to stop talking in class, sit elsewhere. You are spending a great deal of money and energy to attend school, and you do not want it wasted just because you cannot hear the lecture. Socializing has its own time and place. Good friends will understand and learn quickly not to be distracting.

Expect the Unexpected.   Instructors may hurry through the last few minutes of a lecture. Be prepared and stay in your seat until you have recorded everything. Often, tests, projects, or reading assignments are mentioned at the end of class. Ask the instructor not to erase the board until you have recorded everything you need to. If you think you have missed something, ask questions.

Knowing that instructors sometimes ramble, be aware and do not lose interest. The speaker may move quickly back into the lecture, and you might find yourself lost if you have not paid attention. Know that some professors give pop quizzes; be prepared for this by keeping up to date with study and review.

Create Questions.   Write down questions that relate to the lecture or reading. For the answers, see your instructor, research class materials, or ask your study group members. Even if you think of questions but do not write them down, thinking of questions will keep you involved and focused on learning.

Find New Ways to Study Math*

Math Is an Entirely Different Animal.   In most courses, you are successful because you read the assignments, study, understand the information, and then pass the tests. Math is different because you must prove your knowledge base through application. You not only have to understand the formula, you also must be able to work out *any* problems associated with it.

Math is different because it is linear in format. Each new concept you learn builds on the ones previously learned. If you skip a class and miss the material presented, you may not be able to understand the next lecture. Once you have fallen behind, catching up becomes difficult.

To be successful at math, you must understand each new mathematical theory before you can proceed to the next one. This understanding comes from doing your homework, working through problems, and striving to understand the basis of each mathematical step. You cannot walk out the door, forget what you have learned, and hope to be successful on the next test you take.

College-level mathematics courses are more difficult than high school math courses. Instructors teach faster and expect you to learn in one semester what it took you one year to learn in high school. It is your responsibility to keep up and to learn the information as fast as it is being presented. Here are some tips for doing that.

Study with a Partner.   One of the best ways to counter math class difficulties is to find a classmate to study with. Your study partner should be someone you can call when you are stuck on a problem and with whom you can schedule regular weekly meetings. This will economize on your study time and may make working through math problems easier and more enjoyable.

Have the Right Skills Before You Begin.   If you have chosen a math course that requires an extended mathematics background and you do not have the appropriate skills, reconsider. If you are placed in the wrong prerequisite math course and fail it, you may not pass the next math course. It is usually better to pass a lower-level math course with an A or a B than to make a C or a D and risk the possibility of failing the next math course taken.

Students who have not attended college in ten to fifteen years may find that over time their former math skills, however excellent, have deteriorated. To ensure a good grade on your first math test, you must have the basic skills you had when you finished your last math class. You can refresh these skills by reviewing old math tests or by working through problems in the review sections of similar textbooks. You might want to hire a tutor if you require further assistance. It is imperative not to delay, because waiting will make it harder to catch up. Tutorial support is most effective when begun within the first two weeks of class.

Conquer Math Anxiety.   Math anxiety, or the attitude "No matter what, I will never understand math because I hate it," dooms you to struggle because you are defeating yourself before you even start. Many academic support centers have tutors trained to assist you with math anxiety. In addition, there is software on the market that can create personalized prescriptions for your specific math problems to ensure a higher level of success in your courses.

---

*This section, "Find New Ways to Study Math," is reprinted with permission from *Winning at Math,* by Dr. Paul Nolting, © 1991 Academic Success Press.

QUICK CHECK

Are you currently taking a math or science class? List three ways that you study differently for them than you do for other classes.

1. _____

_____

_____

2. _____

_____

3. _____

_____

_____

Review the Text Before Starting Homework.   Review all textbook materials that relate to your homework before you begin. This saves you time in the long run. If you are not able to work out a problem, you might have a better chance at re-membering the location of a similar problem if you have reviewed already.

Also, review all of your lecture notes that relate to your homework before you begin. If you are not able to follow textbook explanations, use your notes for clar-ification, or call your study partner.

Complete Homework Neatly.   Do your homework as neatly as possible. If you have a question for your instructor, before or after class, he or she will be able to see what your previous attempts at solving the problem were by looking at your work.

Overpractice.   Practice problems repeatedly until you are confident in the proce-dures needed to do the problem and any versions of the problem correctly. In study groups, time each other and see how accurately you can work problems. No-tice how long it takes you to complete the problem. The time constraints simulate the classroom testing situation and help you know prior to a test how much time each problem will take. The more you prepare and practice, the less anxiety you will experience on tests.

Even If You Can Do a Problem in Your Head, Write It Down.   Write down every step of the math problem, even when you can do the problem in your head. This may take more time, but the overlearning process will improve your memory and help you on future tests. Doing every step is an easy way to memorize and understand the material, and it also provides you with a complete model of the problem for future study.

Reworking problems you had wrong allows you to identify where you made the error and is well worth the effort. Use a different-colored pen or pencil for corrections.

If you do not understand how to do a problem, use the following steps:

1. Review the test material that relates to the problem.
2. Review the lecture notes that relate to the problem.
3. Review any similar problems, diagrams, examples, or rules that explain the problem.
4. Refer to another math text, math computer program, or math video to obtain a better understanding of the material.
5. Call your study partner.
6. Skip the problem and contact your tutor or math instructor as soon as possible for help.

Understand Before You Proceed.   Understanding is more important in math than memorization. Do not memorize how to solve problems; instead, know the reason for each step. When similar problems are presented on a test, you will want to know the rules, laws, or properties that are needed to solve each problem.

Finish with Success.   Do not quit or give up. Always finish your homework by successfully completing as many problems as you can. Even if you get stuck, go back and try to complete the assigned problems before quitting. End your home-work experience on a positive note. Feel good about your accomplishments.

Write What You Learn.   After finishing your math homework, take a moment and write down what you have learned. This information will increase your ability to learn new math concepts. Place the writing in your math notebook, and then quickly review it at the beginning of your next math class.

Do Not Commit Academic Suicide.   Do not get behind in class or in your homework. It is academic suicide. If you miss class, or do not practice the problems, you will not be able to understand what the instructor is talking about. Getting behind in math is the fastest way to fail the course.

Study Science More Effectively

Many of the math study tips also apply to science. However, studying science may be a different challenge, depending on your interests and academic background. If you have chosen science as your major, you will probably see these courses as fun and challenging. If you are taking science as credit for graduation and feel like you need a little help, then the following tips are for you.

Choose a Science Course That Fits Your Interests, Experience, and Abilities.   Take charge of your education by making smart choices when you plan your semester schedule. Examine course descriptions and prerequisites in the college catalogue before you enroll. Go to the bookstore and evaluate the assigned textbook so that you know what the course will entail before you begin.

Science courses like astronomy, biology, and earth science emphasize learning information. Chemistry and physics emphasize problem solving. Students who have a strong math background may prefer chemistry or physics. By reflecting on the type of science you like, you can choose a course that is compatible with your experience and interests. If you are currently in a class that you know is too difficult, talk to your advisor to discuss alternatives.

Do Not Let Your Attitude Stop You Before You Start.   Choose to have a positive experience in each classroom that you enter. Your image of what science might be is probably different from the reality. When you think of science, do you think of peculiar smells, terms you cannot understand, or professors who look a little different? Let go of your negative perceptions and start fresh. Each time you notice thoughts such as "I do not understand" or "This is confusing," take charge by reading more slowly, rereading, asking questions, seeking tutoring, or setting up more study-group time. As you learn, doubt and frustration will disappear. Remember, you control your learning by managing your attitude and your studying behaviors.

Learn to Pronounce and Understand Science Terminology.   Terms in science may be lengthy, unfamiliar, and difficult to pronounce. They can be daunting when previewing a chapter or even reading one paragraph, yet tests are often based on them. Therefore, it is important to spend extra time slowly reading each paragraph. Break paragraphs into small sections, making sure that you are understanding what you are reading. Science is not a course where you can skim pages and hope to learn information quickly. By correctly pronouncing the terms, correlating terms to definitions, creating note cards, and studying in groups, you can learn science more easily.

Compare and Contrast Graphs, Illustrations, and Appendixes to Your Reading. Reading alone may not be enough. Use graphs and illustrations to complement your reading. Be sure to spend extra time understanding graphs and illustrations because they often make concepts clearer than words. The idea that a picture is worth a thousand words is especially true for science. Graphs and illustrations may be easier to recall than specific terms.

Appendixes in your text support lectures and readings. They often provide chapter summaries, answers for end-of-chapter quizzes, classifications and tables, or additional graphs or techniques that support your current learning strategies.

Make the Most of Science Labs.   The classroom and reading assignments provide theoretical scientific knowledge. The labs allow you to practice what you have learned from lectures or readings. Always try to understand the relationship between lectures, readings, and lab assignments.

Resist the urge to skip lab and do it later. The time you miss from labs can be difficult to make up and may cause you to lag behind in handing in homework or understanding the application of theory.

Ask questions before you start the lab. Make sure you know what the purpose of the experiment is and what procedures you should follow before you begin.

Write an outline of your lab reports in an organized, neat format before you leave the room. If you wait until you go home, you might forget important, specific points that should be included. If your notes are messy or difficult to read, you may not be able to interpret them. Always proofread and reread lab assignments before handing them in.

Use a Computer to Support All Study Techniques

Your computer can increase your organizational ability and improve your capacity to learn. You can store information, create your own study guides, type study questions, compose an analysis of information you have already learned, and use CD-ROM study aids to enhance and support your current study strategies.

Store Data.   By storing significant information on files in your computer, you will save time and be more organized. With the dates for significant projects or exams recorded on your computer-generated calendar, you will have easy access without having to remember where you put your daily calendar. You can even scan handouts from instructors to keep in easily accessible files for retrieval. Use your computer to store any information relevant to your study sessions.

Create Study Guides.   After reading an assignment or listening to a lecture, you can create your own study guide of terms, definitions, and formulas that will support your study efforts.

Create Practice Tests.   Practice tests are a good way to study. Whether alone or in a study group, after reading your assignment or studying your notes, create a computer-generated test. Include questions and problems in different formats (e.g., true-false and fill-in-the-blanks) and be sure your test covers all of the material for which you are responsible. By using computer graphics, different fonts, italics, and bold, your review process becomes easier and more fun.

Type to Learn.   After studying, sit at your computer, pick a topic, and type anything about it that comes to mind. Through free-writing, you can assess how much you know and how much you still need to learn while simultaneously reviewing each topic.

Use Educational CDs.   Educational games are available that will reinforce concepts and offer an opportunity for fun. You can work at your own pace and choose your level of learning.

Surf the Internet.   When you are stuck and cannot find the answer to a question, access the Internet, where there are hundreds of thousands of accessible resources. Cruising the Net is an enjoyable way to enhance and reinforce your studies. Be

QUICK CHECK

List three Internet addresses that correlate with the courses you are taking now.

1. ....

....

....

2. ....

....

....

3. ....

....

....

aware, however, that some Web sites are more credible than others. When reading information from the Internet, do not forget to use your critical thinking and problem-solving skills to assess its accuracy. If you choose a site from a nationally known organization or publishing company, you can be more confident of the accuracy of the information. When in doubt, ask your instructor.

Practice Study Strategies

The purpose of this exercise is to integrate and practice various study strategies.

1. What study strategies do you use currently that are not mentioned in this chapter? Why do these strategies work for you?

    a. _____

    _____

    b. _____

    _____

    c. _____

    _____

2. List three new study strategies discussed in this chapter that you will use. Try them for three consecutive study sessions and then write about their strengths and weaknesses.

    a. _____

    _____

    _____

    b. _____

    _____

    _____

    c. _____

    _____

    _____

    _____

3. Find a graph or illustration in one of your current textbooks. Copy it and attach it to this exercise. Explain in your own words what the graph or illustration is trying to explain, what you learned from this graph or illustration, and how this graph or illustration enhances your understanding of the information presented in the text.

_____

_____

_____

_____

_____

_____

_____

Memory

QUICK CHECK

Think of a lecture that you attended last week. On a separate sheet of paper, write down everything you remember from it. Now reread your notes from that lecture. What percentage of information could you remember?

Studying daily, reviewing, and using PQ4R are some of the best ways to learn. Because studying is not simply memorizing, your method of learning should allow you to understand information. If an idea or concept is to be stored in long-term memory, it must be imprinted intensely in your mind. If imprinting does not occur, forgetting may be the thief of your hard work.

In an experiment, people were asked to read a textbook chapter and then were asked how much they remembered. The respondents forgot 46 percent of the material within one day, 79 percent after fourteen days, and 81 percent after twenty-one days (Pauk 1997).

Reading seems to promote memory retrieval more easily than the spoken word. If you read, you can recite, stop, reflect, and read again. If the words are spoken, it is harder to recapture them. This concept was exemplified by an experiment done at the Cambridge Psychological Society. Researchers secretly recorded a seminar in which the members had participated. Two weeks later, the members in attendance were asked to write down what they remembered. They could not accurately recall more than 10 percent of the points that had been presented in the lecture. Much of what participants remembered was different from what was actually presented, and in fact, incidents were remembered that had never occurred. Casual remarks were exaggerated, and specific pieces of information were reported that had been alluded to only (Pauk, 1997; Hunter, 1957).

The Curve of Forgetting

Hermann Ebbinghaus (1850–1909) was a pioneer in the study of human memory. One result of his research was the curve of forgetting: the longer the time lapse after learning information, the harder it is to retrieve the information. He discovered that our memory for learned information is best directly after a learning session. He found this by presenting a list of nonsense syllables (e.g., dod, gid, eoe) to his only research subject, himself. He used nonsense syllables because they were meaningless and seemingly would be more difficult to remember. He was hopeful that he could identify a "pure" memory that was not tainted with meaning or compounded by earlier learning (Davis and Palladino, 1994).

Ebbinghaus's studies have been supported by further research, including that of Jenkins and Dallenbach (1924), who discovered that memory loss correlates directly

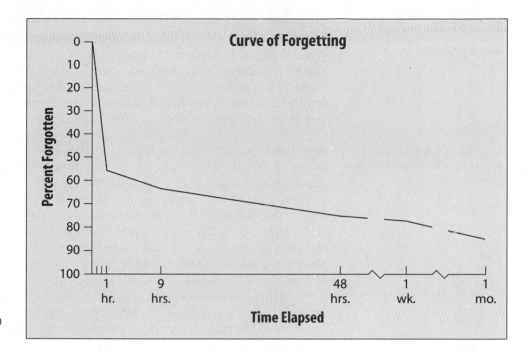

Curve of Forgetting

Percent Forgotten

Time Elapsed

Source: Reprinted by permission from Atkinson, R.H., and Longman, D.G., *Reading Enhancement and Development,* Third Edition. © 1990 West Publishing Company.

with the amount of time elapsed. This theory is further reinforced by the Curve of Forgetting figure by Atkinson and Longman. More than 50 percent of information is forgotten after 1 hour and 70 percent is lost after 48 hours. (Davis and Palladino, 1994; Jenkins and Dallenbach, 1924; Curran and Keele, 1993).

The research illustrates that with the passage of time human beings forget things. This is why some students proclaim that cramming works. They cram as much information as possible into their brains prior to an exam, regurgitate the information, then leave the room, and forget most of it. The goal of learning is to store information relatively permanently, not simply for tests. Cramming stores information only for a very short period of time. Since you are in college to learn information for your career and your life, cramming seems to defeat your purpose.

In order not to forget, you must make an effort to remember. Repeated study sessions, visualization of concepts, and overlearning fight forgetfulness.

Mnemonic Devices

MNEMONICS are simple associations, rhymes, or aids used in remembering.

Mnemonics are simple associations, rhymes, or aids used to prompt memories. When you want to remember something, by using a mnemonic you send a recognizable cue to your memory bank that in effect calls up or prompts the needed information. Mnemonics force you to associate what you are trying to remember with what you know already.

If you have a great deal of information to learn quickly, mnemonic devices can serve as a memory retrieval cue, but they should not be used as a substitute for learning and understanding. Before you create and use mnemonics, be aware that it can take more energy to create and remember the mnemonic than it does to learn the original concept. Be sure to put mnemonic devices into perspective and realize that memorization without understanding is superficial. Examples of mnemonics are coding, acronyms, and acrostics.

CODING changes information in ways that make it more memorable.

Coding.   Information that is not meaningful or relevant to the learner is hard to remember. Coding makes information more memorable by translating it into a more meaningful form. If you had to remember BIR, WOC, and MIR, it could be difficult because they lack meaning. For easier memory retrieval, you could code them in reverse. Then BIR becomes RIB, WOC becomes COW, and MIR becomes RIM, which are familiar and easy to recall.

An ACRONYM uses the first letter of key words to encourage memory retrieval.

Acronyms.   An acronym is a word or group of words created by using the first letters of key words to help you remember a concept—for example, MADD (Mothers Against Drunk Driving) or, in psychology, GAS (General Adaptation Syndrome, a theory that discusses an individual's ability to adapt to stress), or HOMES (a way to remember the five great lakes: Lake Huron, Lake Ontario, Lake Michigan, Lake Erie, and Lake Superior). Practice memorizing the acronym and then reciting what each individual letter represents to prevent confusion and memory loss at test time.

An ACROSTIC is a sentence or phrase built from the first letters of key words.

Acrostics.   Acrostics are sentences or phrases built from the first letters of key words. If you are learning a concept that must be remembered in a specific order, acrostics work. Acrostics use the letters of the key words to form a sentence. What is the sentence "Every good boy does fine" an acrostic for? Every Good Boy Does Fine is familiar to many piano students as the way to remember the lines of the treble clef: E, G, B, D, and F. The sentence "Please Excuse My Dear Aunt Sally" helps students to remember that the order of math operations is the following: Parentheses, Exponents, Multiplication, Division, Addition, and Subtraction. To learn the angle of a triangle, use SOH-CAH-TOA, which will help you remember Sine = Opposite over Hypotenuse, Cosine = Adjacent over Hypotenuse, and Tangent = Opposite over Adjacent. By reciting an acrostic and thinking about it, the concept will be stored in your long-term memory more easily.

ASSOCIATION is connecting a concept you are trying to learn with a memory that is already established.

Association.   Associating a concept that you are trying to learn with a memory that is already established is a quick way to remember information. The association of "lefty—loosey; righty—tighty" when you are trying to turn on a water faucet can prevent confusion or frustration. Names are difficult to remember. The more you can associate a name with a picture, rhyme, song, or image of someone with the same name, the easier it will be to recall the name when you see the person again. For example, if you meet Robyn for the first time, you could start singing the song lyrics "Rockin' Robin, tweet, tweet . . . ," and if nothing else, the embarrassment would help you recall her name the next time you see her.

        When other forms of study cannot help you retrieve information from memory, mnemonics can provide easy memory triggers. They do not take the place of learning or understanding, but they do provide helpful ways to remember.

QUICK CHECK

Which memory trigger works best for you?

....

....

EXERCISE

Memory Triggers

The purpose of this exercise is to practice using memory triggers as a study technique.

1. Work in groups of four and list examples of coding, acronyms, acrostics, and association that are not in this chapter. You may need to research this further on the Internet or at the library.

    a. Coding:

_____

_____

_____

b. Acronyms:

_____

_____

_____

_____

c. Acrostics:

_____

_____

_____

_____

d. Association:

_____

_____

_____

_____

2. Which technique was the most effective? The least effective? Why?

_____

_____

_____

_____

_____

_____

_____

Step Inside . . . The Academic Support Center

The Academic Support Center, the office that provides academic support to students, may be called the Academic Resource Center, the Student Accessibility Center, the Teaching Learning Center (TLC), or the Learning Skills Center. Whatever the name, all college campuses provide support to their students in offices manned by tutors, volunteers, professors, or professionals. These people are trained in diagnosing and helping students with learning or other disabilities; helping students who are learning English as a second language; tutoring; teaching study strategies; and answering academic questions.

The Academic Support Center conducts tutoring and minilectures on most subjects taught at your college. When you become frustrated with your studies, instead of giving up or yelling at the dog, contact the support center. Many have walk-in tutoring, while others require appointments. Some students visit the center biweekly or more often to increase their understanding of specific subjects. It is free of charge, and its sole purpose is to help students become successful as they meet various academic challenges. If, for example, you walk out of a math class and feel confused or frustrated by the lecture, you can walk right into the academic support center and set up an appointment for tutoring so that you can alleviate your frustration and improve your confidence that you do know how to work out the problems.

Some academic support centers have hotline phone numbers so they can answer your questions twelve to eighteen hours per day. Other centers provide on-line service so that you can receive help from the comfort of your own home via your computer.

Internet Exercise

Look up study skills on the Internet and find two Web sites that describe study strategies. The links may be connected to topics such as effective study skills, the ten best study skills, study traps, successful learning, using the Academic Skills Center, and so on. List the address, author, title, and summary of each site:

1. Web site address:

   Webmaster/author:

   Title:

   Summary/description:

2. Web site address:

   Webmaster/author:

   Title:

   Summary/description:

Role Play   Leonard

Break into groups of four to five, and read aloud the setting and role play. Your task is to create the ending of this role play through discussion and collaboration in your group. You may change the dialogue and add new characters. Your role play conclusion should demonstrate that you have reflected on the character's perspective and his circumstances. Then, act the role play out for the class. After each group has acted out its role play, discuss the questions that follow.

Setting: *Leonard Gohl, an adult planning to return to college, and Martha Goode, head of student recruitment, meet in Martha's office.*

Leonard is thirty-seven years old. For the past twenty years, he has worked as a manager for a large food chain. The company downsized, and he was forced to leave. Leonard has set aside some of his severance package for tuition and textbooks. He plans to work part time and attend college classes. Leonard is a single parent raising two teenage sons, Troy, 15, and Jeff, 13.

Martha is twenty-six years old. She is head of student recruitment and head of the orientation program for returning adults.

Leonard: [*To himself, while waiting for Martha to appear*] What am I doing here anyway? This is crazy! I am just too old to be going to school. [*Sees Martha coming*] Oh, don't tell me this is the head of recruitment. She could be Troy's date for homecoming. I'll just go through the motions of the interview and then get out of here.

Martha: Hello, Mr. Gohl. Sorry about being late. I had to get your high school transcripts.

Leonard: Those are ancient history.

Martha: Well, they go back a bit, but they're not prehistoric.

Leonard: Miss Goode, to tell you the truth, I don't know why I'm really here. Looking around the campus, I feel so old and out of place.

Martha: That's a natural feeling. Most returning adults feel that way.

Leonard: I'm here because I lost my job. It is from no great love of learning.

Martha: Well, that is one of the reasons many adults return to school. I know you will not believe this right now, but many of them start to really enjoy coming back to school.

Leonard: I don't think I'll be one of them.

Martha: Why not? What are some of your concerns about returning to school?

Continue the dialogue. Allow Leonard to express his concerns. Incorporate Martha's responses to those concerns, including study strategies he could use to be an effective learner.

Questions

1. Into what stereotype has Leonard cast himself?

2. What type of lifestyle adjustments will Leonard and his sons need to make when he returns to school?

3. How can Leonard help himself to feel more comfortable in the college classroom? What kind of study strategies should he use?

4. What can instructors do to ease the tension a returning adult student feels?

Review

This review is correlated with the objectives at the start of the chapter. One way to study Chapter 4 is to look at the objectives, write down everything you learned about each one, and then compare your notes to this review.

1. *Reading strategies can be improved with PQ4R.* **P**review: Go over the material to get a quick grasp of the information before reading or listening to lectures. **Q**uestion: As you preview or read the chapter, write questions in the margins or in your notes. Questions will encourage thought. **R**ead: Actively read the assignment. **R**eflect: Ponder, contemplate, and rethink information. **R**ecite: Read the assignment aloud; hearing your own words is a powerful learning tool. **R**eview: Going over and over materials eliminates the need for cramming and increases understanding.

2. *Master basic study strategies.* Make an extra effort to remember information, create interest in the subjects you study, learn general concepts first and then learn more specific ones, manage time wisely, study the hardest subject first, overlearn, create effective study sessions, narrow down information to be studied, be a kinesthetic learner, review notes immediately after class, stay focused when studying, study when you are energetic, and visualize your lessons.

3. *Control your study environment.* Study in the same area, choose your study area carefully, choose a well-lit study area, and have supplies available before you begin.

4. *Prepare for the classroom.* Read notes before class, monitor your attention, attend all classes, keep a positive attitude, listen and participate, sit in the front of the classroom, make sure that your friends are a study support—not a study distraction, expect the unexpected, place marks next to notes that will need further clarification, write or ask questions, and use memory triggers.

5. *Find new ways to study math.* Math is presented in a linear fashion, with each concept building on another. Find a study partner, have the right math skills for the courses, ask for help, review the text before you start homework, complete homework neatly. Write down every step of a problem, understand the first step of a problem before proceeding to the next one, and finish math assignments on a positive note. Write down what you learn from each assignment and do not get behind in class or in your homework.

6. *Study science more effectively.* Choose a science course that fits your interests, experience, and abilities. Go to the bookstore and evaluate the assigned text before you start classes. Choose to have a positive experience. Learn to pronounce and understand science terminology. Compare and contrast graphs, illustrations, and appendixes. Try to see the relationship between lectures, reading, and lab assignments. Always proofread and reread lab assignments before handing them in.

7. *Use a computer to support all study techniques.* A computer can increase your organizational ability and improve your capacity to learn. Create study guides and practice tests, compose information analysis, and use CD-ROM study guides to enhance your study sessions. Access the Internet to increase your knowledge of the subject. Always use your problem-solving and critical thinking strategies to assess information on the Internet for accuracy.

8. *The curve of forgetting.* The result of Hermann Ebbinghaus's research is that the longer the time lapse after learning information, the harder it is to retrieve it. In order not to forget, you need to overlearn and make an effort to remember. Cramming stores information only for a short time; studying to learn allows you to remember for your career and your life.

9. *Mnemonic devices.* Memory triggers, including coding, acronyms, acrostics, and association, serve as retrieval cues.

Note-Taking

By the end of this chapter, you will be able to ...

1. Diagnose your note-taking style, learn how to improve it where needed, and implement techniques that work for you.

2. Understand how listening enhances note-taking from lectures.

3. Identify your instructor's teaching style and know how it affects your notes.

4. Learn note-taking techniques for texts and lectures—such as the outline format, the Cornell format, the diagram format, and the note card format—and understand which one works best for you.

5. Take notes in labs effectively.

The purpose of the following checklist is to help you diagnose the effectiveness of your note-taking.

Check the appropriate answer:

1. Are your notes still understandable when you reread them? YES _____ NO _____

2. Do your notes include memory triggers for test preparation? YES _____ NO _____

3. Do your notes prepare you adequately for tests? YES _____ NO _____

4. Do your notes help you understand concepts? YES _____ NO _____

5. Do your notes indicate what material is important to know? YES _____ NO _____

6. Do your notes organize the material for you? YES _____ NO _____

7. Does taking notes keep you more focused during lectures? YES _____ NO _____

8. Do your notes reflect good listening skills? YES _____ NO _____

9. Do your notes state specific facts (dates, names, quantities, dimensions observed in lab)? YES _____ NO _____

10. Does your note-taking style change based on the complexity or simplicity of the information presented or the instructor's style? YES _____ NO _____

If you are a successful note-taker, your answer to most of these questions will be yes. If you said yes to most or all of them, write the reasons for your success.

_____

_____

Write about the questions you answered no by recording specifically what you need to learn from this chapter to improve your note-taking. Remember that your note-taking strategies are good or you would not have gotten this far in your educational career. Marking no means that there are areas in which you need to practice or try new note-taking strategies.

_____

_____

College is a whole other ballpark as far as school work goes. The professors assume that students are educated, and prepared for class. They quickly whip through the materials, allowing one to write only what is really needed, while trying to store the rest of the material into the memory bank full of unneeded memories like what Frank Thomas hit in his rookie year. It is only my strong note-taking skills that get me through this onslaught of information.

Joshua Hjorth, student
ILLINOIS STATE UNIVERSITY, NORMAL, ILLINOIS

NOTE-TAKING means writing down what you want to remember in a format you can follow later.

Notes help you retain information and organize thoughts and ideas. Whether you are in a lecture hall, a science lab, or the library doing research for a paper, effective note-taking is very important.

Note-taking means writing down what you want to remember in a format you can follow later. Important concepts can be difficult to retain in your memory, no matter how interested you are or how hard you try. Notes are crucial not just to test-taking but also to learning and to understanding lectures and texts. Good note-taking skills are important on the job as well.

Notes are not just written words. They can be drawings, colored diagrams, flowcharts, sentences, paragraphs, or outlines. Good note-taking is *not* a haphazard process. Writing notes is purposeful. It helps you learn and retain a wealth of information, increases your focus and attention, and keeps you involved actively in reading a textbook or listening to a lecture. Notes can help you work effectively in study groups. You can correlate your own notes with those of other study group members, to check their accuracy and to fill in the gaps.

This chapter presents several note-taking formats with which you can experiment. It will help you learn the most effective and workable techniques for taking notes in lectures and labs and while reading. Notes are effective if they work *for you*.

First, let us analyze your current note-taking style—what works and what does not—and adjust it wherever necessary.

Examining Your Current Note-Taking Style

It should be obvious that to take good notes you must pay attention to the lecture and record what you hear. What is more difficult is deciding what to record and which format to record it in. If your notes suffer from any of the following common flaws, read on.

What If My Notes Are Confusing?

Whether you use an outline, sentence fragments, or key words, the important question is, When your notes are a few hours or days old, will you still be able to understand what you wrote as well as its significance? If you do not understand your own notes, what is the purpose of writing them down in the first place?

Effective Notes Are Created Through a Purposeful, Organized, Focused Effort.

You can make your notes more understandable by doing the following:

▶ Write at the top of the notebook page the date and the page or number of the chapter you are covering.

▶ Write numbers on all notebook pages in case they become separated from each other.

▶ Number theories or concepts as you record them. Use subtitles or an outline format where appropriate to help clarify the presentation of a mass of information.

▶ Type your notes, either during class or afterward. The typing process will provide you with notes that are easier to study because they are easier to read. Some students use laptop computers during lectures to ensure accuracy and to increase their speed in note-taking. (Some instructors may not allow this; know the rules for each class.)

▶ Leave blank lines to add details and clarification later. Go back and fill in the lines with additional information that you remember or want to correlate with the reading assignment.

▶ Review the notes shortly after taking them.

How Do I Know If My Notes Are Comprehensive Enough?

Did you provide yourself with enough information in your notes to

▶ Remember and understand what the lecturer meant?

▶ Retain important information about concepts, definitions, problems, formulas, or theories?

▶ Reflect the essence of what you have been reading and studying?

If not, you can improve the situation by focusing on facts. Perhaps you need to write down more than you are doing now by seeking out actively what you may be missing: during a lecture, ask questions; when reading an assignment, reread; before a lab, prepare a list of what you need to record and then fill in the details.

What If My Notes Do Not Prepare Me for Tests?

Do you study your notes faithfully only to find that you are still not prepared? If so, you can increase your note-taking skills as follows:

▶ Study the last test and compare the questions you missed to the notes that you took on that specific topic to see where the gaps were and how you can improve your note-taking.

▶ Ask the instructor questions to clarify any confusing areas in your notes.

▶ Ask the instructor to look at a couple pages of your notes to make sure that you have recorded the correct information.

▶ Correlate the words in your notes to commonly used words in the text or the lecture, thus enhancing your understanding of concepts instead of mechanically memorizing terms or definitions.

▶ Write and study your notes for application in real life. For example, in a business course you might ask, "How does this theory apply to a business in which I am the manager?"

▶ Take notes that are focused on the specific content presented by the instructor. Do not allow yourself to get lost in generalities.

When you feel that your notes are not preparing you effectively for tests, do not give up. By using the preceding techniques, changing your note-taking style, paying more attention to detail, and asking for help from classmates, tutors, or instructors, you will become more successful in note-taking and test-taking.

What If My Note-Taking Style Seems Ineffective?

One reason for this is that note-taking styles may need to change for different courses. The notes you take in algebra will be different from the ones needed for anatomy. For example, algebra notes are detailed, step-by-step notes, whereas in anatomy a sketch with labels may be enough. Notes in a literature class could be more free floating than those in a physics course.

Note-taking style often changes with the amount of information you already know. If you are familiar with lecture materials, note-taking is less laborious. If the material being presented is new, complex, or confusing, your notes may need extensive detail. This chapter presents various note-taking formats that you could use. You may find that the diagram or note card format is appropriate in some situations and that the Cornell or outline format is appropriate in others. You may need to find one note-taking format that you can adjust or use different formats for different situations. As you read about various note-taking styles in this chapter, decide which ones will suit note-taking for specific classes.

Recording Notes from Lectures

Listen Attentively

The first step in taking good notes from lectures is to listen attentively. That means paying explicit attention to all communication cues: body language, voice, language, and eye contact. Here are some suggestions for increasing the amount of useful information you can gain through attentive listening.

How do you keep yourself
focused when taking notes?
© Susie Fitzhugh.

Focus on Words and Their Meaning.   Words have symbolic meanings that can be different for different people. When you listen to a lecture, what meaning do the instructor's words have for you? Is your interpretation correct? Distorting the meaning of the instructor's words can contribute to the learning of wrong information. Your judgments and opinions can impair your ability to understand the instructor's viewpoint. Suspend them. Focus on the here and now—listen first, take notes on what you hear, and only later evaluate what has been said. As you listen, quietly ponder, challenge, think critically, and question what is being said in order to understand the meaning of the words. When unsure, ask questions or look up the concept in the text for clarification.

Be sure to pay special attention and record notes when the instructor says, "Please remember," "Please note," "Pay attention to," "The six steps are," "Facts you need to know," and "Do not forget." Use a star or check to signify an especially important point. Later, when you review your material, you will know the areas on which to spend the most time and energy.

Ask Questions to Clarify Meaning.   The best communication goes two ways: back and forth between communicators. Most instructors want to explain concepts so that you will understand them and will not leave the classroom confused. Therefore, ask questions to understand and learn. This is called *feedback*. It is likely that several other people in the classroom have the same question, so do not feel embarrassed to ask. When your questions have been answered, record the specific explanation in your notes.

FEEDBACK refers to receiving information from others that encourages understanding.

Be Aware of the Instructor's Nonverbal Messages.   Messages without words can be a very strong mode of communication. Watch body language: an instructor's excitement about teaching certain topics may be communicated nonverbally. His or her animation can be a clue to the relative importance of the point being made and help you answer the question, Will this be on the test?

Keep Eye Contact with the Instructor.   The more you watch the instructor, the easier it will be to listen carefully to what is said. It should also prevent you from falling asleep! One thing is certain: you cannot take good notes if you do not listen. Another important factor in good note-taking is understanding how the instructor's teaching style affects your ability to record comprehensive notes.

It is necessary when taking notes to become familiar with
the individual professor's lecture style. Learn to take hints
and suggestions from [your professors]. Whether class notes
are casually jotted down or done in a formal outline form, the
most important point to remember is, if you're not in class,
you can't take good notes.

Roberta Freeman, student
WESTERN WYOMING COMMUNITY COLLEGE, ROCK SPRINGS, WYOMING

Adjust Note-Taking to Your Instructor's Lecture Style

QUICK CHECK

Which teaching style works best for you?

....

....

....

....

....

....

TELEGRAPHIC NOTES are brief memoranda with no unnecessary words.

Style refers to the instructor's energy level, body language, eye contact with the audience, and use of props like boards, computers, and overheads. Style can also describe the relationship that the instructor builds with you and the other students in your class. One instructor might rush into a room and move swiftly from podium to board, projecting high energy. Another instructor may use every bit of energy just to speak loud enough for you to hear. This type of instructor may never stray far from the podium and may show little or no enthusiasm. A third may be somewhere in between.

Some instructors place emphasis on factors that will help you learn the materials more effectively. These instructors will often provide an outline of the lecture, grant extra time for note-writing, emphasize and reiterate main ideas, use examples, write important dates on the board, and explain the goals of the lecture. Other instructors impart great quantities of information without doing any of these.

The instructor's style can affect the way you take notes. The high-energy instructor might be easier to take notes from because you are kept awake, unless he or she speaks so fast that you cannot keep up. The low-energy instructor might not be able to keep you motivated. Understanding that the teaching styles of instructors affect the way you take notes can help you consciously change your note-taking style.

Experiment with notes to identify when you should use short telegraphic notes rather than long, detailed notes. Listen, understand, and then write in the briefest format possible. Make sure, however, that your telegraphic style does not lose the meaning because you shortened the information too much. Full-length sentences are appropriate when the concepts are confusing or important. You might use telegraphic writing when the psychology professor says, "The stimulation of the lateral hypothalamus will cause the start-eating center to be destroyed, creating an aphagic or very skinny organism, because it does not know when to start eating." A telegraphic format would be "destroy lateral hypothalamus = skinny rat = aphagic = does not eat."

Use symbols in ways that have meaning for you. Be aware that similar symbols mean different things in different courses. Take "O," for example: in biology O means female; in flowcharts O means connector; in math O means circle; in stamp collecting O means used; and in weather classes O means clear (Grolier, *Encyclopedia of Knowledge,* 1995).

Students in large classrooms can prevent distraction and increase learning by focusing, listening, and then using appropriate note-taking formats.
© Andrea Burns.

Create your own symbols for commonly used words. Here are some examples:

4	for		R	are		C	see
ok	okay		B+	before		Y	why
EZ	easy		U	you		–	negative

Use a wavy line (~) to indicate "ing."

work~	be~	hear~	help~	shovel~

The nature of the lecture or the lecturer often guides you in this note-taking style selection. A fast-speaking instructor presenting complex information will require explicit attentiveness and telegraphic notes. An instructor who has a less intense teaching style might allow you to become more relaxed in your note-taking style.

Alter your note-taking style to adjust to the instructor's teaching style by using the following suggestions:

▶ When your instructor does not start the lecture with a list or explanation of goals for the lecture, try to create your own based on what you have read about the topic and on lecture content, and incorporate it into your notes.

▶ When you cannot hear the instructor, or if the instructor speaks too fast or does not allow adequate time to record notes, ask the instructor to speak louder and slow down. Sit in the front of the class to hear better. Do not let your notes suffer because you are afraid to make changes or ask the instructor to repeat information.

▶ When you are not sure what the instructor means, do not record confusing notes. Instead, ask the instructor for a more detailed explanation during or after class.

▶ Experiment to identify when you should use telegraphic notes versus long, detailed notes.

Y ou cannot set limitations on whom you can learn from.
You must also be willing to learn from a person whom
you dislike.

Cathy Bowman, student
CENTRAL CAROLINA COMMUNITY COLLEGE, SANFORD, NORTH CAROLINA

Adjust Note-Taking to Your Learning Style

QUICK CHECK

How does your current note-taking format correlate with your learning style?

....

....

....

....

....

There are many different note-taking techniques. It is up to you to choose the one that works best for you.

Think back to Chapter 1. What was your identified learning style? Relate your learning style to a note-taking format that works best for you. If you learn best by hearing, know that listening is your key to note-taking success and write down only those concepts that you know you will not remember through hearing alone. If you learn best through visual cues, then you may need to pay more attention to overheads or board notes. If you learn best through hands-on experience, then you probably look forward to lab classes or study groups where you can put theory into action. You may want to experiment with the following popular and successful note-taking formats until you find one or two that match your learning style.

Source: Adapted from *Grolier Encyclopedia of Knowledge.* Copyright © 1995 by the Grolier Educational Corporation.

OUTLINE NOTE-TAKING MODEL

I. Biosphere
  A. Area able to provide sustenance for life
    1. Thin expanse extending 5 to 6 miles above the planet's surface
    2. Pattern of organism's growth dependent on water, light, altitude, and soil composition
    3. Temperatures between 9° and 36° F
  B. Energy Flow
    1. Earth has hot and cold spots—heating and cooling unevenly—causing convection currents
    2. Energy balance is essential to maintain life
      a. Global transfer of energy from areas of excess heat (equatorial regions) to areas of minimal heat (polar regions)
      b. Motion of the oceans also transports energy (North Atlantic Gulf Stream carries warm tropical waters north)
II. Technology Alters Biosphere
  A. Since the Industrial Revolution, technology has endangered the biosphere
    1. Degeneration of land, water, and air
    2. Mineral resources depleted
    3. Acid rain/global warming
  B. Solutions
    1. Creation of "Green Groups"
    2. Environmental Protection Agency is working on long-term plans to prevent further destruction

Note-Taking Formats

Outline Format

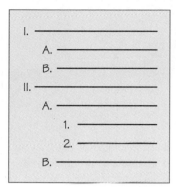

Outlines list main ideas and follow them with minor ideas, enabling you to quickly differentiate the two when reviewing. Usually, an outline includes the main idea, then a supporting minor idea, and then details, which can be followed by even more specific details.

The outline format is efficient if your learning style is focused on details, numbers, and organization. Outlining lets you place your notes in an organized format when you are in class, saving the extra time it would take to reorganize them later. Because you are using numbers and sentence fragments, you can record essentials quickly. This format allows you to focus more on the lecture and less on the note-taking process.

Even if you do not write an outline in your notes, you could create an outline later using your computer. If you use software that has an outline feature, you will be able to scroll through the text and code every heading in your notes to create an outline. This process allows you to organize your notes while reviewing them.

Another way to review from an outline is to look at the major concepts, cover the minor ideas with a piece of paper, and see what you can remember without peeking. Continue to work through all of your notes until you feel comfortable in your knowledge of the materials. If you have never used this format, it may be awkward at first. But with practice, you will become more comfortable.

EXERCISE

Outline Note-Taking Format

The purpose of this exercise is to practice using the outline note-taking format.

Examine the Outline Note-Taking Model, and then choose a class in which to use the model to take notes. Always state the main idea first to reinforce the focus of your notes as you write. Be sure to include specific details that will enhance your learning.

Cornell Format

Psychology	A science that studies behavior and mental processes.
Models of Treatment for Abnormal Psychology	1. Physiological 2. Psychodynamic 3. Cognitive 4. Sociocultural 5. Behavioral

The Cornell format allows you to create a review sheet while taking notes. Draw a vertical line from the top to the bottom of a page of notebook paper. Leave two or three inches to the left of the line. This space is for terms and questions. The right column is for definitions, summaries, and answers correlating to data on the left.

The Cornell note-taking format works best if you need structure as you take notes. The line helps you focus on the content and correlates content with the terms, theories, or formulas that you must learn. If you have a less focused learning style, you will find this method helpful when preparing for a test. You can fold the edge of your paper to create a study guide. With the answers hidden, test yourself on the more detailed facts written on the right-hand side.

When you are taking a test, try to visualize the words on the right and left side of your notes. Your note-taking format can serve as a visual memory trigger that helps you choose the correct answer on the test.

CORNELL NOTE-TAKING MODEL	
(MAIN IDEA) Abraham Maslow's Hierarchy of Needs	
Five levels (from lower level to higher level)	1. Physiological needs 2. Safety and security needs 3. Love and belonging (social needs) 4. Esteem needs 5. Self-actualization
Physiological needs	Survival needs: air, food, water, appropriate body temperature, avoidance of pain
Safety needs	After meeting physiological needs, people look for security in their lives. This could include living in a safe environment, job security, medical insurance, or anything that would protect their physiological needs.
Love and belonging (social needs)	After meeting their safety needs, individuals look to meet their social needs through love, friendship, and belonging to social groups.
Esteem needs	After meeting social needs, interest moves to the need to be recognized, feelings of self-confidence, self-respect, status, and prestige.
Self-actualization	After meeting all of the previous needs, individuals work to reach their own potential, including the ability to be creative, reach self-generated goals, and feel competent in life.

Source: Adapted from B. Reece and R. Brandt, *Effective Human Relations in Organizations.* © 1996 Houghton Mifflin Company.

EXERCISE

Cornell Note-Taking Format

The purpose of this exercise is to practice the Cornell method of note-taking.

Examine the Cornell Note-Taking Model, and then choose a class in which to use the model to take notes. The first step is to draw a vertical line and list terms or questions on the left side and the corresponding theory or answers on the right side.
Remember that you can use these notes as a review sheet when studying for tests.

Diagram Format

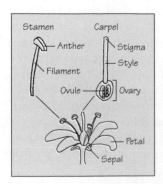

If you find it difficult to stay focused on a lecture, draw pictures or diagrams that illustrate the instructor's ideas. It may not be the most conventional method, but if it works for you, use it.

Drawing diagrams is most effective in classes where you find writing words to be difficult or confusing, classes in which pictures are more effective than words, or classes that are just plain boring. Of course, you can combine the written words with your pictures to emphasize and clarify ideas.

Even if you take your lecture notes in the Cornell or the outline format, you may want to draw diagrams as well. Use colored pencils or markers later to highlight the diagrams you created in class for better retention and retrieval of test data. A visual image will trigger your long-term memory.

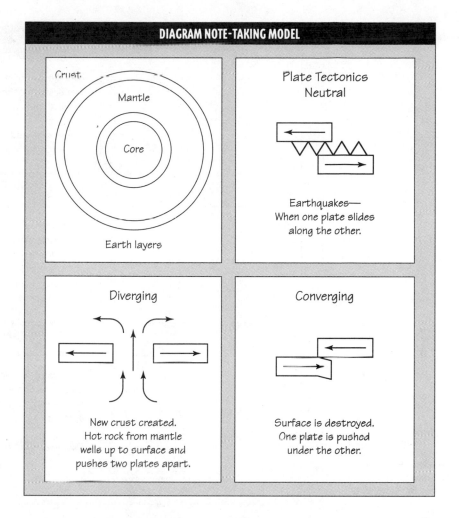

Source: From *1001 Things Everyone Should Know About Science* by James Trefil. Copyright © 1992 by James Trefil. Used by permission of Doubleday, a division of Random House, Inc.

The diagram format is an advantage if you learn best by doing and seeing. If you are a visual learner, you may find in test situations that the diagram will be easier to recall than the written format. The act of drawing the concept may make it easier for you to learn. Remember: Looking at a diagram is different from drawing it yourself. The more you practice drawing diagrams, the easier it becomes.

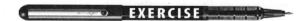

Diagram Note-Taking Format

The purpose of this exercise is to practice the diagram method of note-taking.

Examine the Diagram Note-Taking Model, and then choose a class in which to use the model to take notes. Use as many diagrams as you feel necessary, making sure that they are detailed and understandable.

Note Card Format

Gustatory	The sense of taste

No matter what your learning style, note cards or index cards can be useful for refining your notes. Writing notes in class, copying them to note cards, and then reviewing them as often as possible will increase your memory retention. Record, rewrite, review, review, review, and review. It is difficult to forget information after going through this process.

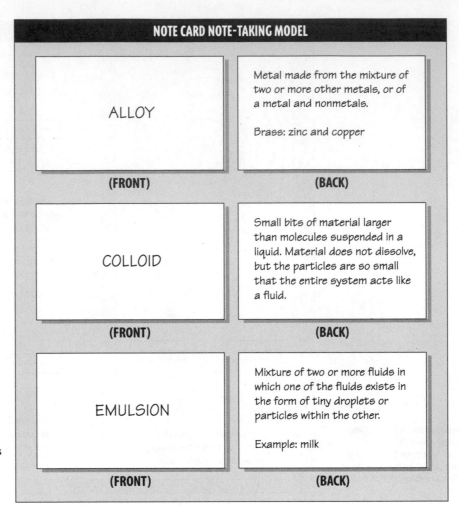

NOTE CARD NOTE-TAKING MODEL

ALLOY (FRONT)

Metal made from the mixture of two or more other metals, or of a metal and nonmetals.

Brass: zinc and copper (BACK)

COLLOID (FRONT)

Small bits of material larger than molecules suspended in a liquid. Material does not dissolve, but the particles are so small that the entire system acts like a fluid. (BACK)

EMULSION (FRONT)

Mixture of two or more fluids in which one of the fluids exists in the form of tiny droplets or particles within the other.

Example: milk (BACK)

Source: From *1001 Things Everyone Should Know About Science* by James Trefil. Copyright © 1992 by James Trefil. Used by permission of Doubleday, a division of Random House, Inc.

QUICK CHECK

List two ways that you like to study with note cards.

1. ....

....

....

2. ....

....

....

Note cards are wonderful; they fit into pockets, briefcases, and purses. There are many ways to use note cards—be creative!

▶ Use different cards for different concepts.

▶ Write a term, formula, or name on the front of the card and a related definition, problem, or theory on the back.

▶ Pull out the cards and study wherever you are and whenever you want—for example, while waiting at the doctor's office or standing in line at the bank.

▶ Color code your cards, using a different color for each subject to visually separate your materials.

▶ Use thin-tip markers to write formulas, charts, terms, or concepts in different colors.

▶ When studying, write any question for the instructor on a note card. Ask questions from the cards before or at the start of class.

▶ Place a note card with hard-to-remember terms on the refrigerator or mirror. By constantly seeing the posted concept you will remember it.

▶ Use completed note cards in study groups as a guide for quizzing each other.

▶ Do not let note cards interfere with your social life. Remember to put them away once in a while to talk to friends and family.

▶ Remember: Put a rubber band around each set of cards in case you drop them!

Note Card Note-Taking Format

The purpose of this exercise is to practice taking notes with note cards.

Examine the Note Card Note-Taking Model, and then choose a class in which to use the model to take notes. Use 3″ × 5″ cards to complete this assignment.

Tape Recorders in the Classroom

Proper Classroom Etiquette Demands That You Ask Your Instructor for Permission to Use a Tape Recorder in Class.

If you are unable to take notes for any reason, then a tape recorder is a great solution. Shut the tape recorder off when unrelated material is being presented. As soon after class as possible, listen to and edit the tape. Delete information that is not needed, and enhance areas that are weak. This process is similar to editing your notes after you write them.

It may also be appropriate to use a tape recorder when you have an instructor who talks very fast. The recorder can pick up any information that you may have missed. Another study technique that you can use with tape recorders is to record information that you want to remember (terms, definitions, formulas) and then, when you are doing other tasks around the house (washing the dishes, working on the car), listen to your prerecorded tape until you are sure that you have learned the taped information.

Keep in mind one disadvantage of using the tape recorder in class to take notes: some students report that they do not listen as carefully because they assume they can depend on their tape later on. Listening is an important requirement for learning, and only by listening can you ask intelligent questions when you need to. Also remember that you always run a risk of mechanical failure. Check your tape, plug, and batteries often.

Recording Lab Notes

You have probably had several years' experience listening to lectures and recording notes. However, you might find that the traditional format used in lectures will not work in a lab. When you are taking notes in biology, chemistry, computers, electronics, language, or medical labs, for example, you may need to

▶ Use more abbreviations.

▶ Write shorter sentences.

▶ Use diagrams.

▶ Record what you see instead of writing down what you are told.

▶ Write more details.

▶ Record cause and effect.

The two most important words to remember when creating lab notes are *what* and *why*. They will be helpful to you as you narrow down the subjects presented in labs and incorporate them into your notes. Always record the date, class name, and topic with the correlated chapter number in the textbook. This will save you hours when you try to correlate lecture, chapter, and lab notes later.

When taking notes in lab, write telegraphic sentences, use diagrams, and record in detail what you see.
© Jonathan Nourok/PHOTO EDIT.

LAB NOTES MODEL

Date _____

Class   (Biology, chemistry, physics, computers, etc.)

Topic and Chapter No. _____

WHAT? (Create a title for each new subtopic you study in lab.)

- What did you learn both generally and specifically in lab today?
- What is most important to remember about this topic? (Be specific.)
- What is the objective of this lab?
- In what ways does the lab correlate with the lecture?
- What will you need to remember from this lab?
- What did you observe, hear, or learn that will help you integrate concepts learned in class?
- What can be done differently to change the final results of the lab?
- In what ways does that change relate to your lecture notes? Tie this change into your notes for easy recall of lecture information.

WHY?

- Why are you conducting this lab experiment?
- Why did you use this particular format, material, or reactants?
- Why is this experiment important?
- Why did you observe your specific result?

ADDITIONAL NOTES: (Add any information that is not included in the above questions.)

EXERCISE

Practice Taking Notes in Lab

The purpose of this exercise is to practice taking notes in a lab in an organized, efficient manner.

Examine the Lab Notes Model. Then select a lab and use this format to take notes. Remember to include more abbreviations, shorter sentences, more diagrams, and more specific details than you would in a lecture class.

Date _____

Class _____

Topic and Chapter No. _____

WHAT? (Subtopic) _____

WHY?

ADDITIONAL NOTES:

Recording Notes from Readings

Recording notes from textbooks and other readings is similar to taking notes in class. The major difference is that textbook note-taking is more closely related to the reading process.

It is always best to preview and read a chapter before writing notes from the text. This means skimming the chapter with special emphasis on headings, sub-headings, and so on (see the Preview section in Chapter 4). The value of previewing is that you may not be familiar enough with the material to know what is important, and previewing helps you determine this. It helps you estimate before reading what the main ideas are.

Should you mark notes in books? Some instructors feel the only way to really know a book's contents is to mark the book, bend the pages, and use it until it falls apart. Others believe a book should never be marked and should be kept in a clean condition. Also, they feel you may spend so much time in marking the book that you miss important concepts and details.

Many people use a colored highlighting pen to bring attention to important points while reading. If you do, be careful that you do not highlight every sentence; that makes highlighting pointless.

In the end, only you can decide how best to take notes from your book.

A LEARNING DISABILITY is an intellectual handicap that interferes with learning.

Step Inside . . .   The Office for Students with Disabilities

Note-taking is a challenge. When taking notes is complicated by learning disabilities, it is important to seek support and information about the services offered on your campus. Knowing your legal rights and where to find help can make the achievement of academic success easier. Learning disabilities refer to specific disorders correlated with talking, reading, comprehension, listening, writing, spelling, or math.

The Americans with Disabilities Act (ADA) became a law on July 26, 1990. It prevents discrimination against people with any kind of disability. If you have a learning or physical disability, you should notify your college so that its staff can offer you the support you need.

Most colleges need proof of a disability prior to offering support services, so be prepared to provide it. Recent documents from your high school or last college attended may be accepted. If not, ask to be tested through their office or request a referral. If, for example, you have dyslexia (seeing words backward, skipping words, confusing similar letters like b/d or p/b), you might need to prove the extent of your disability prior to receiving help from the college.

You can submit to your college a list of services that you need based on your disability. The staff wants to know what accommodations can be provided to enhance your success at college (e.g., a quiet room for testing, someone to read a test, wheelchair-accessible tables).

Check your handbook for the specific office on your campus that works with disabilities. The staff will discuss your concerns, provide testing, and offer suggestions to increase your learning and note-taking skills.

Internet Exercise

Locate an Internet site for note-taking. After you have found a note-taking article that is of interest to you, answer the following questions.

1. What are the title, address, and author of the note-taking site?

_____

_____

_____

2. Summarize the contents of this site.

_____

_____

_____

3. Is this site up-to-date? Is it factual? If you said that it is up-to-date and factual, explain in detail your reasons for believing it is accurate. If you said it is not up-to-date and is not factual, list the reasons for saying so.

_____

_____

_____

_____

_____

_____

_____

_____

Role Play Laura

Break into groups of four or five, and read aloud the setting and role play. You will need to create the ending of this role play through discussion and collaboration in your group. You may change the dialogue and add new characters. Your role play conclusion should demonstrate that you have reflected on the character's perspective and her circumstances. Then, act the role play out for the class. Answer the questions after you finish acting out the role play.

Setting: *Laura is sitting in Dr. Gonzalez's lecture classroom.*

Laura is a college freshman. She works part-time as a receptionist at a dentist's office. Her parents have agreed to pay for her tuition as long as she maintains at least a C average. Her books and spending money are her own responsibility. Laura wants to buy a car and is trying to save money by working more than twenty hours a week. Lately, she has become overwhelmed with her studies and work responsibilities.

Dr. Gonzalez is a no-nonsense English instructor. He expects students to be prepared for class and to participate actively during discussion. Lecturing is his primary teaching method.

Laura: [*To herself*] This stuff is so boring. Who cares if Hamlet was really nuts or not? He must have been because I could not understand a word he was saying.

Dr. Gonzalez: [*Walks toward Laura's desk and asks her a question*] So, what motivates Hamlet to have the players put on a scene that depicts murdering a king?

Laura: [*Looks down and hopes Dr. Gonzalez will direct the question to someone else. Notices that her notebook pages are empty.*]

Dr. Gonzalez: [*Waits for Laura's response*]

Laura: I really didn't hear the question, Dr. Gonzalez.

Dr. Gonzalez: [*Addresses another student*] So, what do you think, Mr. Patel?

Laura: [*To herself*] Oh, he never gives you a chance to answer. I know I wasn't listening, but he could have repeated the question.

Dr. Gonzalez: That's right, Mr. Patel. Guilt is a major theme in the play.

Laura: [*To herself*] I can't wait for this class to be over. Only six more minutes of torture. I have to get out of here right away and go to work.

Dr. Gonzalez: Now, are there any questions about Hamlet's relationship to his mother, Gertrude?

Laura: [*To herself*] I do have a question, but I would never ask it. The last time I asked a question, Dr. Gonzalez made a sarcastic crack.

Dr. Gonzalez: That's all for today. Ah, Laura, I'd like to talk to you after class.

Laura: [*To herself*] Oh, no! I just want to get out of here.

Continue the dialogue with your newly created ending. Include both Dr. Gonzalez's and Laura's perspectives.

Questions

1. Describe how a student can succeed in a class that employs the lecture method.

2. What are some of the factors that are affecting Laura's listening and note-taking?

3. How should Laura prepare for Dr. Gonzalez's class?

4. Discuss a personal instance when you have felt frustrated in class. What did you do to correct the situation?

Review

This review is correlated with the objectives at the start of the chapter. One way to study Chapter 5 is to look at the objectives, write down everything you learned about each one, and then compare your notes to this review.

1. *Learn how to improve your note-taking techniques.* Note-taking is not a haphazard process: notes are effective only when they work for you. Constantly evaluate your notes to be sure that you have made the appropriate adjustments for teaching style and accuracy.

2. *Listening enhances note-taking.* To increase your listening powers, focus on words, try to hear without judgment, ask questions if you do not understand the message, look for nonverbal messages, and maintain eye contact.

3. *Identify your instructor's teaching style.* Part of effective note-taking is understanding the instructor's teaching style—his or her energy level, body language, eye contact, use of props, and overheads.

4. *Adjust note-taking to your learning style.* There are many different note-taking techniques. Choose the one that works best for you.

   Outline format: The outline format is a quick, organized way to record data. Numbers, letters, and short sentences are used to record the main points of the lecture.

   Cornell format: The Cornell format allows you to create a review sheet while taking notes. Use a vertical line from the top to the bottom of a page. The left column is for terms and questions. The right column is for definitions, summaries, and answers correlating to data in the left column.

   Diagram format: The diagram format combines the written word with pictures to emphasize ideas.

   Note card format: In the note card format, each card holds a different concept. You can write a term, formula, or name on the front of the card and a related definition, problem, or theory on the back. Review the cards until the concepts are understood.

5. *Lab notes.* When recording notes from labs, use more abbreviations, shorter sentences, and diagrams to record what you see. Asking the questions *What?* and *Why?* helps focus your lab notes.

CHAPTER 6

Test-Taking

OBJECTIVES

By the end of this chapter, you will be able to . . .

1. **Identify and practice general test-taking strategies for essay, fill-in-the-blank, multiple-choice, true-false, and open-book tests.**

2. **Learn ways to prepare effectively for a variety of tests.**

3. **Learn and implement strategies to fight test anxiety.**

TEST-TAKING STRATEGY CHECKLIST

The purpose of the following checklist is to help you understand your test-taking effectiveness.

Check the appropriate answer:

1. Do you scan the test when you receive it to ensure you have the right number of pages? YES _____ NO _____

2. Do you make sure that you write all requested information on the test (name, section, course, date)? YES _____ NO _____

3. Do you take a deep breath, relax, and visualize yourself feeling calm and knowledgeable? YES _____ NO _____

4. Do you listen and pay attention to written and verbal instructions? YES _____ NO _____

5. Do you check the board for additional instructions? YES _____ NO _____

6. Do you read your test carefully? YES _____ NO _____

7. Do you answer questions you know first? YES _____ NO _____

8. Do you mark the questions that you do not know; leave time to go back to them; then answer them accordingly? YES _____ NO _____

9. Do you ask your instructor to clarify directions or questions you find confusing? YES _____ NO _____

10. Do you guess (if it does not count against you)? YES _____ NO _____

If you are a successful test-taker, your answer to most of these questions will be yes. If you said yes to most or all of them, write the reasons for your success. Even if you said yes to all of them, there are always areas that need more work. Write about the areas that you need to work on to improve your test-taking skills.

_____

_____

If you said no to a number of the questions, record specifically what you need to learn from this chapter to improve your test-taking.

_____

_____

P reparation enables a student to feel more relaxed and
   confident during test-taking time. Even the ever-dreaded
finals week can be a culmination of a successful semester
through good planning, proper studying, proper relaxation
time, and good test-taking techniques.

Julie Crombie, student
WAYNE STATE COLLEGE, WAYNE, NEBRASKA

Tests are tools used by instructors to measure students' retained knowledge in specific academic areas. But tests are more than that to students. Tests represent the ability to remember and transport information into various formats. Whether your instructor lectures, shows a movie, or orchestrates small-group activities, it remains important to remember what you learned in each situation. You may be asked to transform that information into speeches, essays, and multiple-choice tests later on. Figuring out the complexities of the testing scenario remains a constant challenge. That is why each test that you do well on, each grade you achieve, each piece of information you remember, and each theory you understand becomes a victory in college. Not only that, but the skills you use in test-taking are the same skills that you will use in your career search and on the job. Each time you learn material for a test, you are also learning for your career. The information learned in college is the foundation of the stored information that you will need to know for life.

Tests measure the number of questions that you answer correctly and what you are able to remember, and illustrate your ability to understand. Tests also force you to learn concepts, theories, definitions, formulas, and ideas by deadlines. What tests do not measure is intelligence, and they usually do not measure creativity or who is the smartest in the class.

Some students like tests and perceive them as a challenge. Tests are a way to show themselves and the instructor that they have mastered new ideas and information. Other students may have an intense dislike for tests and experience anxiety as soon as they are handed one. They can learn to counter their distaste for tests by reviewing and studying smarter.

Put tests into perspective. Tests need to be seen as a way to learn, not as something to pass or fail. An F on a test means that it is time to reevaluate your study and test-taking strategies. Do not let low grades discourage you. Instead, change your behavior. Give yourself control over tests by learning new test-taking strategies so that you can study more effectively.

Test-taking requires preparation and dedication. This chapter will help you to increase your ability to prepare for quizzes, tests, and final exams by learning various test-taking strategies.

Preparing for Tests

There are many ways to prepare for tests: the tried and true ones that you have always used, as well as new ones. As you prepare for tests, incorporate the following suggestions into your test-taking strategies.

Before the Test

Create Practice Questions

▶ As you study, create and write out your own test questions.

▶ When creating questions, see if you can second-guess the instructor. Try to predict questions that the instructor might ask.

▶ Put the questions on 3" × 5" cards and use them as a study guide.

▶ On a daily basis, see how many questions you can answer. Look up those you do not remember.

▶ Study through the pile of cards you have. When you know the answer, take that card from the pile and place it in an "Already-Know" pile. Keep working through the "Do Not Know" pile until you learn the information on every card.

▶ Once you have worked through all of the cards, take out the entire Already-Know pile again and see how many you still remember.

▶ Continue a daily review until the exam.

▶ Review the Already-Know pile the night before the exam.

Review Notes Daily

▶ If you study your notes daily, you will be prepared for the test. You will be able to walk into the test rested, relaxed, confident, and unstressed because you were not up the night before cramming.

▶ Rehearsal of information on a daily basis allows information to transfer from short-term memory to permanent storage in long-term memory.

▶ Use study groups as a fun way to review and learn.

▶ As you study, create memory strategies and visual images to increase information retention.

▶ Concepts that have been consistently reviewed and stored in your long-term memory are much easier to retrieve. Review your notes as soon as possible after completing them.

Get a Good Night's Sleep

CRAMMING is forcing too much information into a tired brain in a short amount of time.

▶ Studying instead of sleeping is not sensible. Lack of sleep interferes with your ability to focus on questions or readily retrieve information from memory. Remember, cramming is forcing too much information into a tired brain in a short time.

▶ If you have reviewed consistently and studied all of the assigned readings and notes, you will not need to stay up all night studying.

▶ If you feel you are not prepared for the test, you will need to make a judgment call. Would you be better off studying for two or three hours and then sleeping? Would you be better off sleeping and relying on what you already know? The decision is your responsibility, but think it through very carefully before you exhaust yourself in the name of studying.

Exercise

▶ Walk, run, hop, skip, or jump.

▶ Exercise before you enter a classroom for a test. When your circulation is moving, you will be more alert and focused as you answer test questions.

If exhaustion has conquered you while you are studying, give in to it. Put the book down, take a nap, and try again later.
© Robert Ginn/PHOTO EDIT.

▶ Exercise enhances an overall good feeling. This good feeling allows you to feel more confident as you complete the test.

During the Test

What Works Best for You in Test-Taking Situations?

QUICK CHECK

How would you describe your test-taking style in ten words or fewer?

▶ Do you like to sit calmly and wait for the test, with your books put away and pen or pencil out?

▶ Do you like to do a last-minute review of notes before a test? (Some students who have short attention spans report that reviewing quickly before a test is helpful. Others say that reviewing right before an exam is confusing.)

▶ Pay attention to your own test-taking style. Use techniques that are effective for you.

You Are in Control of the Test; the Test Does Not Control You

▶ Monitor your thoughts while taking the test; keep them positive and focused.

▶ Relax. Take a deep breath; let your muscles relax; then refocus on the test. This simple process forces anxiety to dissipate while regenerating memories that will supply you with the knowledge needed to do well on the test.

Scan the Test

▶ When you receive the test, make sure that all of the pages are there. Sometimes pages are missing. Instructors may not be sympathetic if you have not answered all of the questions because of a missing page. They may feel it is your personal responsibility to know how many pages there are on the test.

▶ Look to see how many questions are on the test. This may help you gauge your time more wisely.

▶ After you scan the test, start with the questions that you know best.

▶ When scanning questions, you may find memory cues in the other questions that trigger an answer you could not remember. You might even find that an earlier question is answered by a later question.

▶ Another scanning technique is to mark the questions you do not know and go back to them later. Otherwise, you may waste time on the ones you do not know and not have enough time to answer the ones you do know.

Visualize Yourself Being Successful

▶ Remember the notion that positive thinking brings positive results. Focus on what you know. The more you focus on what you do not know, the more anxious you will become and the less you will be able to remember.

▶ Visualize a picture of yourself being confident, feeling comfortable, and knowing the answers. This visualization can increase memory as it reduces anxiety.

After the Test

Ask Questions! If You Do Not Understand, Ask Again!

After completing the test, find answers to questions that puzzled you or of which you were unsure. This immediate reinforcement of learning correct answers will help you understand the correlation between your studies and the instructor's testing style.

▶ Talk to classmates about their answers on the test. The more you discuss test information, the easier the concepts will be to remember for the midterm or final. Be sure to accept other students' answers as correct only after verifying the right answer through the text or with the instructor.

▶ Seek out the correct answers and make sure you understand your mistakes. If you are still confused, ask the instructor.

HOW SHOULD YOU PREPARE FOR TESTS?

BEFORE THE TEST	DURING THE TEST	AFTER THE TEST
Preview chapters before you study.	Pay attention to your test-taking style.	Seek correct answers to questions that were puzzling or confusing.
Find and create visual cues to trigger memory.	Scan the test.	Clarify and understand mistakes.
Review often.	Start by answering the questions you know first.	
Create practice tests.	Mark the ones that you do not know and go back to them.	Pay attention and note correct answers when the instructor reviews the test.
Use 3" x 5" cards for test preparation.	Stay focused.	Find ways to turn low grades into high ones.
Avoid cramming.	If you become frustrated or anxious, turn the test over, relax, refocus, and try again.	If tests become problematic, review Chapter 4, and seek help from support services in your college.
Overlearn to prevent test anxiety and frustration.	Find ways to make a testing situation a positive challenge.	
Ask questions to gain insight and understanding.		

▶ Ask questions; ask questions; ask questions! The more you ask, the more you learn and understand.

▶ Take responsibility for finding ways to change low grades to higher ones. Use pertinent suggestions from Chapter 4 and the test-taking suggestions from this chapter to seek solutions to, not excuses for, grades that you do not like.

Preparing for Specific Testing Formats

Be sure to ask instructors what type of test they will be administering. By knowing ahead of time if a test will be essay, fill-in-the-blank, multiple-choice, or true-false, you will be more prepared. As the next paragraphs illustrate, preparation for different test formats requires different approaches and study strategies.

Essay Tests

Before Taking an Essay Test

▶ Find out how many questions will be on the test and how much time will be available to complete the test.

▶ Study and understand all major concepts. Pay special attention to details that will support the major ideas in your essays.

▶ Learn how to spell relevant terms and the names of relevant people.

▶ If you were the instructor, what questions would you ask? Create essay questions that you think could be on the test. Practice writing the answers. The more you practice, the more confident you will be at test time.

While Taking an Essay Test

▶ Bring an erasable pen to the test. Instructors want to see neatness in your essay tests, not inky, messy blobs.

▶ Before you begin writing, look over the test and note how many questions there are. Pay attention to the points attached to each question, so that you spend the most time on the questions with the most points.

▶ Do not let questions you do not know upset you or make you feel insecure about your knowledge base. Start with an easy question first to build confidence.

▶ If you do not know an answer, start an outline that relates to the question. If an outline fails to bring about an appropriate answer, try a diagram or flowchart. You may find that you know more than you think as you use these test-taking strategies.

▶ Be sure that the first paragraph contains the main answer to the question. Then provide support and explanation throughout the rest of the essay. Include any information that you feel is relevant, especially concepts that the instructor has emphasized in class.

▶ Pay attention to words in the test question that help you understand the instructor's expectations, and reuse these words in your response. For example, if a psychology test says, "List and explain two characteristics of the Type A personality," an answer might be, "Two characteristics of the Type A personality are as follows: (1) Polyphasic behavior. Type A personalities believe that they must do many things at once. For example, they might put on makeup, drink coffee, and talk on the phone while driving. (2) Walk fast. Type A personalities believe

WORDS COMMONLY USED IN ESSAY QUESTIONS

BY UNDERSTANDING THE MEANING OF THESE WORDS, YOU WILL BE ABLE TO ANSWER QUESTIONS PROPERLY.

ANALYZE: To separate into parts and explain.

COMPARE: To evaluate so that you can find similarities and differences.

CONTRAST: To find differences between two or more things that are compared.

DEFINE: To describe exactly; to state the characteristics or meaning.

DISCUSS: To provide opinions on a course of action or an issue.

ENUMERATE: To name one by one in a specific list.

EVALUATE: To find the value or worth.

EXPLAIN: To provide meaning or interpretation; to state reasons for better understanding.

INTERPRET: To make meaning clear with new or different words.

LIST: A series of words, names, or numbers, often presented in order.

OUTLINE: A systematic listing of major and minor ideas or concepts.

SUMMARIZE: To concisely state a main idea, avoiding too many specific details.

that time should never be wasted. They often walk fast so they can quickly move on to the next task" (Friedman and Booth-Kewley, 1987).

▶ Watch the time carefully! The most common mistake made when taking essay tests is spending too much time on one question and not being able to finish others.

Helpful Hints for Essays

▶ Write next to each question the amount of time you think you will need to effectively complete the essay. Then manage your time accordingly. Be sure to wear a watch, or use the classroom clock to guarantee sticking with your schedule.

▶ Remember that instructors want you to recall information, examples, dates, and facts in a format that is in full sentences, organized, and understandable. Use transitions that help the instructor follow your train of thought from paragraph to paragraph.

▶ Read the question several times. Make sure that your writing relates directly to the stated question.

▶ Write on one side of the paper only. The ink bleeds through if you use both sides and makes the paper messy and difficult to read.

▶ Some instructors want you to skip a line as you write. It makes it easier for them to read. Write legibly. You want to know that what you write can be read by the instructor without frustration.

▶ Finish the essay with a summary that tells the reader the main points of the writing while tying those points back into the original question.

▶ Try to leave a few minutes at the end to check for spelling and grammatical errors. Also check the organization of your essay to make sure that the content makes sense.

QUICK CHECK

What are three of the "most helpful" hints for taking essay tests?

1. ....

....

....

....

2. ....

....

....

....

3. ....

....

....

....

Taking Essay Tests

The purpose of this exercise is to provide practice in writing essay tests.

Choose a topic that you are currently learning about in your classes and create an essay question. Answer it to the best of your ability without the use of texts or notes. Then find a partner and critique each other's work.

1. *Topic:*

_____

_____

2. *Essay:*

_____

_____

_____

_____

_____

_____

_____

_____

_____

_____

_____

_____

_____

3. *Peer Critique:*

_____

_____

_____

_____

_____

Fill-in-the-Blank Tests

Before Taking a Fill-in-the-Blank Test

ROTE MEMORY is mechanical memorization.

▶ Remember that this type of test is based often on rote memory, which is mechanical memorization. This means that you must rehearse the concepts until they are stored in your long-term memory. The more you rehearse, the easier the retrieval of information will be on the test.

▶ Review; review; review. Concentrate on reviewing, because your answers will be based on total recall. You will not be able to use associations as you do with multiple-choice questions.

▶ A great tool for fill-in-the-blanks tests is 3″ × 5″ cards. Write the term on the front and the definition on the back.

▶ You are studying specific concepts, not general ones. Look for terms or concepts that you think the instructor could turn into fill-in-the-blank questions. Create your own tests and practice them until you understand the concepts.

▶ Choose specific review times and place them in your calendar. Make sure that you follow through. This type of structured, organized studying will pay off.

While Taking a Fill-in-the-Blank Test

▶ Before answering any of the questions, read each question carefully. Some terms are similar and can be confused easily.

▶ First, answer the ones that you are 100 percent sure are correct. Then go back and answer the rest. Make guesses only if the instructor states that there is no penalty for guessing.

Multiple-Choice Tests

Before Taking a Multiple-Choice Test

▶ Find out how many questions will be on the test. This will help you understand how focused or general your studying should be. If there are only ten questions, and the grading scale is 100 percent, each question will be worth ten points; thus, your study must be focused on specific content areas. If there are fifty questions, the point value for each question will be much less, and your studying may need to be more general.

▶ The instructor's expectations could be different for each test. Be sure to ask questions that clarify the instructor's intentions, and study accordingly.

▶ Study to remember associations. The fact that you can choose from several options in multiple-choice tests allows you the freedom to choose answers that are associated most closely with the right answer.

While Taking a Multiple-Choice Test

▶ A frequent mistake is not paying attention to directions. For example, before you start the test, you need to know if any question has two answers. You also want to know if you will be penalized for guessing. The answer to these concerns would be in the written or oral directions. If you are not sure, ask.

▶ Pay attention to associations. The memory cues are in front of you on the test. Think about each answer and then associate the possible option with what you know is the right answer.

▶ Some multiple-choice questions are created so that you will have to apply learned information to get the right answer. They are not all based on mechanical memorization.

▶ Do not spend too much time on questions that confuse you. Leave them and come back to them later.

▶ Look for terms like *none, always, never, all, sometimes, usually,* and *seldom.* One of these words can change the whole meaning of the question. When you see one of these terms, read the question carefully because they can be misleading.

▶ Negative words can be confusing. Words like *no, negative,* or *not* can change the meaning of the question.

▶ If it is a Scantron test, check it at least twice before you hand it in. Make sure that you have placed your answers in the appropriate boxes. It is easy to look at the number on the Scantron form incorrectly and consequently make mistakes throughout the test.

▶ If you make a mistake on a Scantron form and have to erase, be sure to leave no marks on the form that the machine might misread. You may want to check with your instructor, as some have policies about Scantron erasing (e.g., if you erase, you must ask for a new Scantron form, or if you erase, the instructor may want to make note of erasures).

▶ When reading the answers for the multiple-choice question, you may find that none of the options presented seems correct. It is important to read the question again to see if you know the answer; if you do, then look for it in the options. If you do not know the answer, and you will not be penalized for guessing, then go ahead and give it your best guess. You will probably pick up points by guessing answers that you would otherwise miss completely.

▶ A common mistake made on multiple-choice tests is not reading through the complete question or all possible options.

True-False Tests

Before Taking a True-False Test

QUICK CHECK

List three of your best test-taking strategies.

1. ....

....

....

2. ....

....

....

3. ....

....

....

▶ Go through all materials that you need to learn, and focus on concepts that you feel could be turned easily into true-false questions. Create practice true-false questions and answer them repeatedly until you get them right!

▶ The more you study and feel comfortable with your learning, the easier the questions will become.

While Taking a True-False Test

▶ Know that in order to mark a true-false question true, the whole statement must be 100 percent true. One wrong word can make the entire statement false.

▶ When you read a question with *always, only,* or *never,* the answer is often false. It is seldom that things always or never happen; instead, they seem to occur somewhere in the middle.

▶ When you read a question with *sometimes, often,* or *frequently,* the answer may be true.

▶ If you are not sure about an answer, before you guess, go through the entire test, as you might find that another question answers the one that has you puzzled.

▶ If you are not sure that you should guess on true-false questions, heed the advise of Walter Pauk, author of *How to Study in College,* Fifth Edition (1994).

> Although you have a 50-50 chance of answering a single true-false statement correctly, the odds are not that high for the entire test. In fact, your chances of guessing correctly on every statement decreases geometrically. In a ten-question test, the odds on guessing are against you by more than a thousand to one. If you're unsure of whether to mark "T" or "F" and you're forced to guess, because you are stumped or pressed for time, the odds are in your favor if you choose true over false.

Open-Book Tests

Before Taking an Open-Book Test

▶ Organize your notebook and text for easy retrieval of information.

▶ Write page numbers on your notes. Create a one-page outline and list the topics that you will need to locate quickly. Specify page numbers (notes and text) next to each related topic.

▶ Place paper clips or Post-it notes on your text for quick retrieval of information. You could color coordinate the Post-its with a similar color of ink on your outline. This will help you remember where specific information can be found without wasting time searching for it.

While Taking an Open-Book Test

▶ Time management and organization are the key to success. Go through the test and quickly create a time plan. Allow enough time to complete the test, to review what you wrote, and to revise.

▶ Answer the questions that you know best, first.

▶ If you cannot find information on a specific topic, come back to it later.

▶ Do not allow yourself to waste time looking for answers on low-point questions when a larger-point question might have information readily available.

Take-Home Tests

You may use the concepts related to open-book tests if you have a take-home test. Do not make the mistake of thinking a take-home test is a "freebie." Take-home tests are designed to be comprehensive, and an excellent grasp of the material is a must. The more you have organized yourself, your text, and your study materials, just as you would for an in-class open-book test, the easier your take-home test will be. Be sure to use a word processor so that the paper you hand in is neat and organized.

Give yourself the luxury of a quiet place to take this test, where you will be free from interruptions and temptations that may distract you (for example, the radio, the TV, the children, and the refrigerator).

Predicting Test Questions

The purpose of this exercise is to predict questions that might be on a fill-in-the-blank, true-false, multiple-choice, or open-book test.

Choose a class in which you will be taking a test. Get together with three classmates who are preparing for the same test. Each person will create six questions—two fill-in-the-blank, two multiple-choice, one open-book, and one true-false. Answer each other's questions. This not only provides an excellent review but also helps you predict and understand what questions might be on the test from a variety of perspectives.

Studying for Final Exams

Final exams are the culmination of what you have been working toward all semester. By starting your semester knowing that daily you are reviewing for the final, you will eliminate the need to cram the night before your big exam.

Finals evoke positive and negative feelings. You feel positive because you are at the end of the term and are successfully completing it. Feelings could be negative because the final might represent 35 or 45 percent of your total grade, causing self-doubts or fear. If you have used the study techniques you learned in Chapter 4 and in this chapter, you will not need to be fearful of finals.

Another way to feel more comfortable before a final exam is to try to find out from your instructor the general and specific guidelines for the materials that will be covered on the final exam. Which chapters, movies, lectures, notes, concepts, formulas, or theories will be on the final exam? Some instructors provide final exam study guides. By getting these early and working with them often, you will be better prepared for finals.

Go over the tests, quizzes, notes, and note cards that you have taken or recorded throughout the semester. These are great review materials as you prepare for the final exam. Review your notes from the text, movies, presentations, or class discussions.

Final exams can be difficult. You may have as many as two or three in one day. Time management and consistent reviewing are necessary when preparing for these important tests. Do not let your final exams scare you. Remember that you control your reaction to your tests. Make final exams a challenge and a victory, not a fearful experience.

Strategies to Combat Test Anxiety

QUICK CHECK

List three ways that you deal with test anxiety.

1. _____

2. _____

3. _____

For some students, test anxiety is a troublesome barrier to achieving good grades. Just by thinking that each grade must be high, you are focusing on performance rather than on learning. Though positive goal setting is good, experiencing test anxiety is proof that you are placing too much attention on performance and not enough on understanding.

Test anxiety may cause you to forget the information that you studied or cause you to feel faint, dizzy, or lightheaded. There are many ways to deal with test anxiety.

Think Positively

Some concern helps motivate you to prepare for tests appropriately. But excessive concern breeds anxiety, and anxiety can halt or prevent effective test performance. So study hard, visualize yourself being successful, and then think positively and confidently as you work on your test. Acknowledge self-fulfilling prophecies. If you *think* you will do well, chances are you will.

Reduce Anxiety Through Preparedness

Walk into tests so prepared that you will have no reason to feel anxious.

Change Perceptions That Cause Fear and Anxiety

When you have physical symptoms of anxiety, it is because you perceive tests as harmful. Remind yourself that you are taking control of the test and have nothing to fear. Then face your fears. Why do tests cause you anxiety? After you answer this question, take a few deep breaths, relax, and strive to put your fears into a positive perspective. This process often causes fears to dissipate.

THOSE WHO FAILED BUT REALLY DID NOT

ALBERT EINSTEIN was thought to be mentally challenged. He spoke falteringly until he was nine. One teacher suggested that he drop out of school.

SIR ISAAC NEWTON was a poor student. His parents permitted him to go to school because he failed at running the family farm.

PABLO PICASSO was removed from school at ten years of age because he was doing poorly in school.

R. BUCKMINSTER FULLER built his geodesic domes by starting with an intentionally failed dome and making it stronger and better through learning from mistakes.

Source: Adapted from "Humbling Cases for Career Counselors" by Dr. Milton E. Lareson from *Phi Delta Kappa,* February, 1973 Issue, Volume LIV, No. 6, p. 374. © 1973.

WHAT DOES AN F MEAN?

IF F MEANS FAILURE TO YOU, THEN YOU MUST CONFRONT THAT PERCEPTION AND CREATE NEW ONES. FOR EXAMPLE, F COULD ALSO MEAN:

Finding help and guidance to master information retrieval.

Focusing on understanding the concepts you missed on the test.

Following tips the instructor gives you for future success.

Figuring out ways to improve your ability to take tests.

Fanatically reviewing texts and lecture notes to find out why you made mistakes.

CHANGE THE WAY YOU TAKE TESTS BY ASSUMING CONTROL OF THEM THROUGH YOUR NEW PERCEPTION OF F's.

Reduce Anxiety Through Writing

When you find yourself anxious before tests, take a few minutes to write down all of the perceived reasons for your fears. You may find that you are giving more power to the test than you should. The writing process will help you understand that some of your fears might be unrealistic. After you write down the thought, write down if the fear is based on reality. Acknowledging the fear behind your test anxiety is the best way to eliminate it.

Use Relaxation Techniques

When you start to feel lightheaded or have heart palpitations, take a deep breath and relax. You may find the following progressive relaxation steps helpful:

1. Breathe deeply from your stomach three times.
2. Roll your neck around from side to side slowly.
3. Imagine your neck muscles relaxing, then your shoulders, back, arms, legs, and feet. Rotate your feet in circles three times.
4. Acknowledge that you are relaxed, that you feel calmer, and that you do have the ability to do well on tests.
5. Whenever physical signs of anxiety return, go through these steps again.

Use Visualization

Visualization allows your thoughts to move away from anxiety and fear. Instead, you can focus on being relaxed and on the task of remembering answers to test questions.

▶ When you see a test question and you are not sure about the answer, try to create a picture in your mind that could answer the questions. (Visualize the page it was on in the text, the graph next to it, or the joke the instructor made about it.)

▶ Often, visualization will allow you to remember graphs, specific notes from the board, pictures, or even definition boxes from texts. This memory lets you answer the questions correctly and gain more confidence as you work through the test.

▶ Visualize yourself remembering the answers.

▶ Visualize places in the text that contain answers to questions on the test.

▶ Visualize yourself in your study area studying the concept. (Often, this mental picture will trigger traces of memory that will bring the answer into consciousness.)

▶ Visualize yourself in the classroom taking notes on this concept.

EXERCISE

Combating Test Anxiety

The purpose of this exercise is to help you understand the situations and perceptions that increase test anxiety.

Finish the following sentences to help you understand what part test anxiety plays in your life. If you do not experience test anxiety, complete only the last sentence. Break into groups of three to five students and discuss your answers.

1. I experience test anxiety when

_____

_____

2. When I experience test anxiety, I feel

_____

_____

3. I combat test anxiety by

_____

_____

4. I do not experience test anxiety because

_____

_____

Step Inside . . . Peer Study Groups

Why study alone when so many excellent resources surround you in your class-rooms? If you could find a quick, enjoyable way to study, wouldn't you do it? The time to tap into those resources is now. Talk to your peers about forming a study group.

Forming study groups in college is one of the best decisions that you can make. Study groups provide support, friendship, solid academic experiences, and fun. When you cannot make it to class because you are sick, members of the study group will take notes for you. When you cannot decipher words in your notes, call a study group member and ask for clarification. When you do not hear your alarm and al-most miss your study group session on Saturday morning, your study group will call you to join them, and influence you to study harder than you would on your own. When you offer your knowledge and expertise about computers to the group, they in turn offer their expertise in history or biology. It is good to know that in a study group someone else usually has a strength in the subject in which you have a weak-ness. When you are tired of rehearsing terms, who pushes you on? Your study group.

Do not make excuses for not forming a study group. Even though study group members have different schedules (many work, some have children, others run their own businesses), you need to make study group time a priority. The study group will save you time in the long run because five minds work faster than one. They will be your motivator when your motivation is low. They will help you understand con-cepts when you are about ready to give up. They are the ones who will share your joy, reflect on the tough times, and provide mutual understanding as you walk across the stage at graduation. They are the ones who will teach you how to work effectively as a team.

Go ahead, right now. Seek out classmates who are willing to learn with peers, commit to learning, and find a support system that will never be forgotten.

Internet Exercise

Look up "test anxiety" on the Internet. List three ways to fight anxiety that are not mentioned in this chapter. Remember to list the Web site address and the author of each article that you access.

1. _____

_____

_____

_____

_____

2. _____

3.

Role Play   Mario

Break into groups of four or five, and read aloud the setting and role play. You will need to create the ending of this role play through discussion and collaboration in your group. You may change the dialogue and add new characters. Your role play conclusion should demonstrate that you have reflected on the character's perspective and his circumstances. Then, act out the role play for the class. When you have finished, answer the questions.

Setting: *Mario, a college student, has gone back to visit his high school art teacher. They are in her classroom after school.*

Mario is an art major. He does extremely well in all of his art courses. However, he is barely passing English and American history. When he studies, he reads the text and reviews his notes and feels confident that he has learned the information that will be on the test. When he walks into the classroom and starts the test, his mind goes blank, and he cannot remember most of the concepts that he studied. He knows he must get better grades than he has been receiving if he is to feel successful as a college student.

Ms. Conroy is Mario's high school art teacher. She has been a mentor to Mario since he was a high school freshman. Ms. Conroy has always been there for him when he needed any kind of help. She has told Mario to call on her whenever he needs advice.

Mario: [*Enters classroom*] Hello, Ms. Conroy. Are you busy?

Ms. Conroy: Mario! What a great surprise! How could I ever be busy for a friend?

Mario: I don't know. Maybe, now that I'm no longer your student, you don't have time for me.

Ms. Conroy: That's nonsense. So, how's school? How are you doing?

Mario: I'm getting an A in drawing and an A in painting.

Ms. Conroy: That's great. I knew you would do well in college.

Mario: I'm doing well in my art classes, but I'm having lots of trouble with English and American history.

Ms. Conroy: Have you asked the instructors for help?

Mario: I'm sort of afraid to.

Ms. Conroy: You have to ask, Mario.

Mario: I know, Ms. Conroy.

Ms. Conroy: Have you formed any study groups in your classes?

Mario: I don't know anyone yet.

Ms. Conroy: Have you tried to get acquainted?

Mario: Well, I . . .

Ms. Conroy: Have you checked out the study skills workshops at the school?

Mario: No, I didn't know there were any.

Ms. Conroy: Check it out, Mario. There you may find out about test anxiety and how to prevent it.

Mario: Test anxiety, what's that?

Continue the dialogue. Include what Ms. Conroy means by test anxiety. Provide additional advice or study tips for Mario.

Questions

1. What type of learning style do you think a creative person like Mario has?

2. What study techniques would you suggest Mario use so that he can be more successful in American history and English? Which of your suggestions would incorporate his learning style?

3. How can Mario become better acquainted with his classmates so that he can form a study group?

4. What can Mario do to prevent test anxiety?

Review

This review is correlated with the objectives at the start of the chapter. One way to study Chapter 6 is to look at the objectives, write down everything you learned about each one, and then compare your notes to this review.

1. *Test-taking strategies.*

   Before the test: Create practice questions. Do not lose sleep the night before a test. Review notes daily. Exercise before tests.

   During the test: Figure out what works best for you in test-taking situations. Remember that you are in control of the test; the test does not control you. When you receive the test, scan it. Visualize yourself being successful.

   After the test: Take the initiative in changing low grades to higher ones. If you are not satisfied with your grades, take the responsibility for changing your studying strategies. Seek out the correct answers by returning to your text and looking up the answers to the test questions that puzzled you.

2. *Prepare for various tests.*

    Essay tests: Prior to essay tests, find out how many questions there will be and how much time you will have. Study and understand all major concepts, learn the spelling of relevant terms, and create practice tests. When taking essay tests, bring an erasable pen, look over the test questions before you begin, understand what the questions expect you to discuss, and feel confident as you write.

    Fill-in-the-blank tests: Studying for fill-in-the-blank tests is more than rote memory. To do well on them you will need to review, review, and review. Concentrate on reviewing, because your answers will be based on total recall. You will not be able to use associations as you do with multiple-choice questions. Note cards, 3" × 5", are a great tool for fill-in-the-blank tests. Place the term on the front and the definition on the back. You are studying specific concepts, not general ones. Look for terms or concepts that you think the instructor could turn into fill-in-the-blank questions. Create your own tests and practice them until you understand the concepts. Choose specific review times and place them on your calendar. Make sure that you follow through. Answer the questions that you are 100 percent sure are correct. Then go back and answer the rest. Make guesses only if the instructor states that there is no penalty for guessing.

    Multiple-choice tests: Prior to multiple-choice tests, clarify the number of test questions, expectations, and scope of the test. As you study, remember associations. When taking multiple-choice tests, read directions carefully and apply learned knowledge to the understanding of each question. Be aware of negative words because they can confuse you. Look for terms such as *none, always, never, all, sometimes, usually,* and *seldom.* Double-check your answer sheet before handing it in.

    True-false tests: Prior to taking true-false tests, focus on concepts that easily could be turned into true-false questions. Practice by creating your own questions with these concepts and answer them until you are confident with the material. When taking true-false tests, remember that for a true-false question to be true, the whole statement must be 100 percent true—one wrong word can make the entire statement false. Look for words such as *always, only,* or *never;* they often make statements false, whereas *sometimes* or *often* may indicate true statements. If you are unsure whether to mark "T" or "F" and you are forced to guess, the odds are in your favor if you choose true over false.

    Open-book/take-home tests: Prior to taking an open-book test, organize yourself and your materials. Use Post-it notes or paper clips to help you find the information you know you will need. Create an outline for your text, noting the page numbers from your book with each concept. When taking an open-book test, manage your time wisely. Go through the test and make a time plan. Answer the questions you know best, first. If you are unsure of where to find information on a concept, skip that question for the time being, and go back to it later. Do not waste your time on low-value questions if a higher-value question may point you in the right direction. The same concepts apply to take-home tests. In addition, do your take-home test in an environment that is free from distractions.

Final exams: Try to organize your study time so that you can review all new and old information daily for each course. The more you review, the less time it takes to study, and the better you will understand the information for the final.

3. *Prevent test anxiety.* Think positively. Prepare the material. Remind yourself that you are prepared and will do well on the test. Change perceptions that cause fear and anxiety. Reduce anxiety through writing. Before the test, write about your feelings concerning your fear and use this process to determine if your fears are based on reality. Remind yourself that you are taking control of the test and have nothing to fear. Then face your fears. Relax. Turn your test over for a moment, and use relaxation techniques. Visualize the material itself (what the page looked like), you learning the material (where you sat, a joke the instructor made), or you completing the test (find a calm image to bring your anxiety down). Make pictures in your mind to guide you through the test.

Writing

By the end of this chapter, you will be able to . . .

1. **Understand the importance of writing in college and in your career.**

2. **Clarify the specifics of each writing assignment.**

3. **Follow the writing guidelines as you complete writing assignments.**

4. **Understand and implement the steps in the writing process.**

5. **Manage your attitude.**

6. **Learn how to combat writer's anxiety.**

7. **Recognize plagiarism and prevent it.**

WRITING CHECKLIST

The purpose of the following checklist is to help you understand more about writing strategies.

Check the appropriate answer:

1. When your instructor assigns a writing project, do you ask questions for clarification, if necessary? YES _____ NO _____

2. When you start a writing project, do you create a written list of potential subjects? YES _____ NO _____

3. Do you use an outline to organize your writing before you begin? YES _____ NO _____

4. When conducting research, are you diligent in making sure that all recorded data are accurate? YES _____ NO _____

5. Do you use reference books for advice on punctuation, citations, bibliographies, or indexes? YES _____ NO _____

6. Do you use headings or subheadings as a way to keep your paper organized as you write? YES _____ NO _____

7. After you have written and proofread the first draft, do you offer it to others for constructive criticism? YES _____ NO _____

8. Do you combat writer's anxiety by freely writing without censoring? YES _____ NO _____

If you answered yes to these questions, write the reasons for your success. If you answered no to any question, look up that concept in this chapter and see how you could improve your writing skills. Write about skills you need to work on.

_____

_____

_____

_____

_____

_____

Communication through writing is one of the greatest skills you can cultivate in school and on the job. The ability to clearly and precisely convey your ideas can make the difference between a "C" paper and an "A" paper or your ideas in the work force being implemented or overlooked.

Claude Meirthew, student
DeVry Institute of Technology, DuPage Campus, Addison, Illinois

Your written work in college will help you discover that writing is more than an assignment; it is a way of life. Think about all the things you do on a daily basis that involve writing. The papers you write, the letters you send, the reports you create, and the job applications you fill out are examples of writing that is often taken for granted. In each case, you need to know how to place thoughts on paper effectively. Words must be spelled correctly, ideas must make sense, and syntax must be grammatically correct. The success of your writing depends on your knowledge, comfort level, and ability to communicate ideas in written words.

Part of being victorious in college is knowing how to write essays, reaction papers, and research papers. With the completion of each writing assignment, your comfort level and expertise in writing increase. Possessing effective writing strategies can help you get and keep jobs, attain promotions, and achieve career goals. The writing skills that you learn in college carry over to your career. They help you to write organized business reports, letters, and memos that are grammatically correct. For example, it is difficult to get a job without sending out well-written cover letters and résumés. Recruiters often throw away résumés that have spelling errors. Promotions into positions with increased responsibility demand effective writing capability. No one wants a manager who cannot communicate properly in writing.

This chapter presents ways to clarify writing assignments, follow steps for research papers, improve writing, combat writer's anxiety, and prevent plagiarism. The main focus of this chapter is the creation of essays and research papers. However, writing is not only something you do in college but also a great way to communicate, share ideas with others, and express feelings that may not be easy to say.

Writing is a way to make your ideas come alive. Experiment with writing. Practice. You may even enjoy it.

Clarify the Assignment

You have a writing assignment. Your instructor tells you to write a 750-word paper and hand it in next week. You write the assignment down as a priority on your to-do list and go home. As you sit in front of your computer and stare at the blank screen, you wait for the writing to happen. Many ideas pass through your mind, but you do not know where to begin.

The best place to start is with the instructor's original assignment. What type of paper has been assigned? Whatever the assignment, make sure you understand the instructor's expectations. Each instructor will expect different things; by asking the right questions, you will understand more easily what you need to do.

► Is your paper supposed to be historical, autobiographical, biographical, theoretical, or scientific?

► Should your paper be informative, persuasive, informational, or research oriented?

► Is your paper based on fact or fiction?

► Will your instructor provide you with the topic, or must you pick one? If you are allowed to pick one, do you need to have it approved by your instructor?

► How many sources will you need? How do you cite them?

► How long should the paper be?

► What are your instructor's overall expectations for this assignment?

By clarifying the expectations of the instructor, you will find fewer roadblocks as you write. Most instructors want papers that are typed double-spaced, neat, and well organized with no spelling errors. In order to be creative in your writing endeavors, it is important to allow your creative juices to flow and not limit your writing with self-doubts.

Writing Guidelines

The following writing guidelines provide support and a basic foundation for your writing effort. As you write, use the guidelines as a gentle reminder to complete all of the steps of writing.

► Choose a subject.

► Narrow it into smaller topics.

► Write a thesis statement.

► Prepare an outline.

► Write a first draft. Cover all of the topics on your outline. Use headings and subheadings.

► Spell the instructor's name correctly. Use the instructor's correct title (Professor, Mrs., Ms., Mr., Dr.).

► Proofread.

► Ask others for constructive criticism.

► Rewrite the paper (integrate suggestions).

► Check punctuation, grammar, and spelling.

► Be sure your paper is neat, organized, and understandable.

► Proofread, make corrections, and read again for last-minute changes.

► Hand in your final paper.

The following section explains the possible writing steps. Try them and see how they work for you. Writing is different for everyone. After using these steps once or twice, change the order, add new ones, subtract the ones that do not work. That way, you will be able to use the steps within your own writing style. These steps are set up for writing research projects. For writing projects that are not research-based, eliminate the "research" and "research notes" steps. The rest remain the same.

mportant skills are involved in the process of writing a
research paper: researching in the library, reading sources,
taking notes from these sources, and writing the actual paper.
Enough time must be allotted for each stage of the process.
There should also be time to proofread the paper and make
necessary revisions. The result should be a well-researched,
well-written research paper.

Maele Seau, student
COLUMBIA COLLEGE, COLUMBIA, MISSOURI

Writing Steps

Choose a Subject

Imagine that the instructor has asked you to write a research paper, report, or essay based on the environment. What would you write about? Sometimes it helps to create a list of all of the topics related to the subject recommended by the instructor. For example, you might choose to write about the environment. Which topic would you choose? Recycling, reducing waste, deforestation, the effects of the Chernobyl nuclear accident on the environment, polluted water tables, extinction of species, ozone depletion, or global warming? When you choose a subject that you like and that is of interest to you, the writing process seems more pleasant and less daunting.

Narrow the Subject

QUICK CHECK

What subject would be fun or interesting to write about?

....

....

....

How many topics can you list from your selected subject?

....

....

....

....

Most subjects that you choose initially will be very general. You will need to narrow down the subject to make it easier to write about. Otherwise, all of the available data can be overwhelming. It would be frustrating to start researching a subject and find that there are two hundred and forty articles available. Where would you begin?

Narrowing down a broad concept (a subject) into smaller parts (topics), before you begin writing will save you time and leave you less frustrated. When you narrow down your subject into smaller topics, and then choose one topic to write about, you can create a more focused paper.

Let us say, for example, that your psychology instructor assigns a five-page research paper on any theorist in the field of psychology. You could narrow your subject by choosing Sigmund Freud from a list that also includes John B. Watson, Carl Jung, B. F. Skinner, Edward B. Titchener, Carl Rogers, Abraham Maslow, and Wilhelm Wundt. After choosing Freud, you will need to narrow the topic further. You could decide to examine a few Freudian theories like unconscious conflict, dream interpretation, personality development, or psychosexual development. Finally, you could complete the narrowing process by choosing "psychosexual development" as your topic.

Write a Thesis Statement

A THESIS STATEMENT contains one or two sentences that state explicitly the focus of a writing assignment.

QUICK CHECK

Choose a topic.

....

....

Write a thesis statement based on your topic.

....

....

....

....

Before you create a thesis statement, take time to read some sources on your topic, reflect, analyze, and understand the sources that you have reviewed. Write down or type some notes from the original sources (remember to record full source citation data): your reactions to new theory, statistics, or ideas. Your reactions to others' written words strengthen your own writing skills. Trust your own thoughts and reflect upon them.

A thesis statement consists of one or two sentences that clearly state the focus of the writing assignment. It summarizes the main concepts to be presented and lets the reader know the order in which topics will appear in the paper. It is a helpful tool because it can keep you focused as you write. It also gives the reader a brief preview of what will be featured in your writing. The only time you would not use a thesis statement is in fiction or autobiographical writing. If the instructor asks that the thesis statement not be included in the final written paper, you may still want to write one for yourself to keep you focused as you write.

You may find as you write your paper that your thesis will change. The more information that you gather, the more likely you are to change your focus. It is possible that the thesis statement may not correlate to a newly written first draft. If this happens, change the thesis statement so that it reflects the new draft.

Do Research

RESEARCHING means finding materials pertaining to your thesis statement.

Once your topic has been chosen and your thesis statement written, it is time to research. There are many ways to conduct research. Visit your library or investigate options on the Internet to see what kinds of information are available. Although the Internet provides you with a massive amount of information, it will be up to you to check resources in the library to be sure that the data you find on the Internet are accurate and factual.

Take pens, pencils, and a laptop computer (if you have one) to the library with you. In your library, you will find card catalogues, on-line catalogues, computer databases, inter-library loan, and much more.

Do not limit yourself to the written word. Also check out videos, laser disks, tapes, and CDs. A variety of community resources are also available to you. You could contact industries, art institutes, museums, village boards, chambers of commerce, zoos, and so on.

Interviews are a viable source of information. For example, if you were conducting research on the environment, you could interview someone at the local waste management company. Most companies are glad to have staff meet with you, as it is a way for them to market the good things they do. If you are not sure whom to call first, call the marketing or customer service department.

Take Research Notes

When conducting research, it is important that you record accurately *all* of the data pertaining to your sources. You may want to refer to the *MLA Handbook* (Gibaldi, 1995) or the *Publication Manual of the American Psychological Association* (1983) for citation style in your final bibliography. When creating your bibliographic information, remember that whether you find the information in books, journals, abstracts, periodicals, or specialized indexes, or on the Internet, your bibliographical notes should include the following:

▶ Journals and periodicals: subject and title of the article, author's name, magazine title, volume number, date of publication, and page number.

► Books and abstracts: title of book, author's and editor's names, name of publisher, place and date of publication, and page number.

► Internet: subject and title, author's name, and Web site address.

Both the *Publication Manual of the American Psychological Association* and *A Guide to MLA Documentation* (Trimmer, 1998) provide guidance in citing all types of references, including electronic sources.

If you use bibliography cards, one card (3″ × 5″) should be used for each source. You could use different card colors for different sources and number each bibliography card. After you have completed your bibliography cards, create 4″ × 6″ note cards. Find a large space on your desk or floor and fill it with all of the materials relating to your research. Write on each note card a main idea, a summary, relevant details, or a quote that you want to present in your paper. Place a brief source citation on each note card, or indicate the number of the bibliography card listing that source, so that you will not confuse various sources when you start your paper. Another option would be to use computer software that can organize bibliographical information.

Outline and Organize

Now that your research is done, one of the best ways to organize your collected information is to create an outline (see Chapter 5). Like thesis statements, outlines allow you to organize your paper without really writing it. They provide a quick look at whether your paper will flow, and how main and subordinate ideas will fit within the body of your paper. Like thesis statements, outlines can always be changed. However, the fundamental parts of the paper listed in the outline usually remain the same.

Place your notes in a topical order that makes sense to you. Use your notes to create your outline. The headings and subheadings included in your outline (based on the main ideas from your notes) will organize the paper for both the writer and the reader. Even if you eventually remove them from your final draft, they remain an important part of the organizing process.

Write a First Draft

Instructors Have Different Ideas about Outlines. Be Sure to Ask Your Instructor for Guidelines

Using your organized notes and outline, write the first draft of your assignment. Do not let this become a difficult or frustrating process. Record all ideas that come to mind. Do not edit or delete at this point. Just get something down on paper for each main and subordinate idea. This will generate a quantity of further ideas that will help you complete the project. You can always delete and elaborate later. Remember, this is not your final draft.

Write and write and write until you feel that you have filled in your outline with written material. Then go back and reorganize the writing until you are satisfied with the content. After you have done this, leave your paper for a period of at least twenty-four hours. Meanwhile, allow your mind to come up with new creative ideas to improve the quality of your work.

Proofread

Proofread your paper for correct spelling, punctuation, grammar, capitalization, and so on. Then leave it alone for another period of time. Review it again later. If you find no blatant errors, ask someone else, such as a family member, a friend, or a professional in the tutoring center at your college, to proofread it for you.

Seek Constructive Criticism

Others can provide you with pertinent feedback regarding your writing. Many professional writers belong to writing groups in which group members provide positive and negative feedback on each of the members' written pieces. Although it is difficult to hear criticism, comments from others will improve the quality of your writing. Study groups can increase writing awareness and skill. However, to offer group feedback effectively, it is important to focus the responses. One way to do this is to ask group members to respond to your writing by answering the following questions:

1. Does the introduction and conclusion reflect the essence of the entire work?
2. Are the ideas that are presented clear and concise? Are any parts of the writing confusing or in need of clarification?
3. Are more transitions needed? If so, what suggestions would you offer?

By answering these questions, the group can stay focused on the essentials of writing and not get lost in details or in ineffective criticism.

Seek Answers to Questions

There are many places to receive support when writing. Most campuses have writing centers or hotlines for quick questions. You can also receive help through the Internet, writer's reference guides [e.g., *The Rinehart Guide to Grammar Usage* (1993) and *The Chicago Manual of Style* (1993)] or various computer programs. Some academic support centers will also answer questions or help you solve writing problems. Ask your instructor what support services are available on your campus for writers.

Some instructors are willing to look over a draft and provide suggestions. Others like to look at your outline before you begin writing and then review your first draft. This is a good idea if you are unsure initially of your writing.

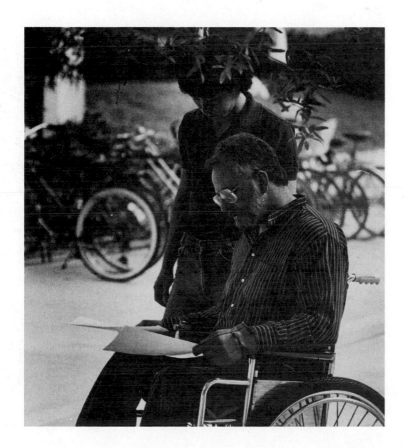

Instructors are interested in supporting your writing endeavors. Be sure to clarify the policy on rewriting outlines, first drafts, and rewrites.
© Spencer Grant/INDEX STOCK.

Students need to realize no piece of writing is ever perfect and that revisions can only help. They should be able to express their thoughts and ideas effectively on paper. This helps students project their ideas clearly to their reader.

Robin Marie Carpenter, student
McHenry County College, Crystal Lake, Illinois

Revise

Make the appropriate revisions and get ready for the final draft. At some point, you have to become comfortable enough with the paper to move on. If you find yourself revising and revising, and never feeling satisfied with your product, stop. Put your paper away for a few hours, and if you find no major imperfections, get ready to write your final draft.

Write a Final Draft

This is it. The end of the road. All of the hours that you have put into this writing assignment will now pay off. Make your final content corrections, and lay the paper aside. Check it later for grammatical errors, awkward sentences, paragraph transitions, and completion of topic coverage. Review the writing checklist at the

By Ruth Flanigan.

beginning of this chapter to make sure that you have effectively scrutinized the entire paper. Make appropriate corrections, and hand it in.

Some students are never happy with the finished product and thus never finish the paper. It may never be perfect in your eyes, but it *must* be handed in. You have given it your best.

Writing Assignment

The purpose of this exercise is to provide you with practice in following the steps for writing assignments.

Choose a subject about which you would like to write a two to three page paper. Narrow the subject. Create a thesis statement. List two bibliographical sources that you will integrate into your paper. Create an outline of your paper, and organize your material. Write the first draft of the paper, ask for constructive criticism (include written feedback in your final paper), revise, and hand in a final draft.

Manage Your Attitude

It is easy to give up on writing when it does not seem to be happening as fast as you think it should. Take a quick break, but do not give up. When you stick with it, the writing ideas will begin to flow. Find ways to keep yourself motivated. Use positive reinforcers when you complete tasks (a walk, lunch with a friend, a sporting event). When you have a thought such as "I will never finish this paper," turn the negative thought into a positive one. Think, "I will finish two pages tonight and then see how much I can do tomorrow night."

Do not be hard on yourself when you write. Creativity comes from the heart and the mind. If you constantly censor your work, you will be stifling your creativity and productivity. Let your thoughts flow, and allow yourself to write.

Know that each time you complete a writing project successfully you are building skills to help you achieve your life goals. Writing is a part of school, of business, and of creativity. Believe in your ability to write and create, learn from your mistakes, and try again. The more confidence you have in yourself, the more confidence will be expressed in your writing.

Combat Writer's Anxiety

WRITER'S ANXIETY is a physical, fearful reaction to any attempt to write.

Writer's anxiety is what you might be experiencing as you stare at the blank screen and try to put your thoughts into words. Your heart might palpitate, and you might wonder to yourself, "Can I really do this?" Writer's anxiety sometimes includes writer's block. That is the experience of feeling that no matter what you write, it is not right, or that no new creative ideas come into your mind as you write. Not everyone experiences writer's anxiety, but if you do, the following tips could help.

Have you ever stared at a blank sheet of paper and not been able to write? Try freewriting! By writing freely without censor, words, ideas, and even paragraphs flow easily.
© Susie Fitzhugh.

Free-writing

Free-writing is writing without censoring. If your mind seems frozen, try free-writing. Sit at the computer, or grab some paper and a pen, and write, write, write. Write for fifteen minutes (minimum) without stopping. Let every idea from the recesses of your mind get recorded on paper. Later, you can edit the information, but during the free-writing experience, no editing is allowed. It is an enjoyable way to unfreeze thoughts and create ideas of which you might not have been aware. This technique combats anxiety because it allows creative ideas to surface without censorship.

Free-talking

If you do not have time to sit and write down your free-floating ideas, then find a tape recorder, and while you are doing the dishes, working on the car, or sitting and enjoying a sunset, record all of the thoughts relating to your topic. Later, as you are writing, you can listen to the tape and take notes on any ideas that pertain to your paper. Free-talking is a great technique for busy people who do not have time to free-write. It also works well for people who create best when not focusing on just one task.

Write Yourself a Letter about Your Topic

This is a technique that gives you permission to write anything you want. It works because you know that no one but you will see it.

Read about the Topic

Record any ideas that come to mind as you read about the topic. Use those ideas later in your paper, remembering to cite sources. By reading and pondering others' ideas, your own creativity can be stimulated.

Change Your Writing Technique

If you are using the computer, take out a pen and paper. If you are writing in sentence form, change to sentence fragments, poems, or rap. This change often sparks new ideas. Just by changing the tools or place in which you write you may find that new ideas can be created.

Take a Break

If nothing else works, leave the writing and do something enjoyable. Go for a walk, work on a hobby, get a good night's sleep. When you return to your writing, the ideas might flow more easily. It is almost as if your brain is working on the ideas while you are physically doing something else. A break provides a fresh start on an old project.

EXERCISE

Combating Writer's Anxiety

The purpose of this exercise is to practice strategies that will decrease writer's block or writer's anxiety.

Choose three of the following strategies, and follow the directions within each one.

1. *Free-writing:* Choose a topic. Free-write for three minutes about the topic without censorship. After you have done this, list the concepts that are good enough to use in a paper.

2. *Free-talking:* Choose a topic. Tape record, for five minutes, all of your ideas about the topic. Create a list of ideas from free-talking that you could incorporate in a writing assignment. Hand in the tape and your written paper.

3. *Write yourself a letter:* Choose a topic that causes you to have mixed emotions or conflicting feelings. Write to yourself about them. What did you learn?

4. *Read about a topic:* Choose a topic. Find a source that relates to the topic on the Internet or in the library. Read for fifteen minutes and then correlate what you read to your topic. Write the correlations on a separate sheet of paper to be included in a writing assignment later.

5. *Change your writing technique:* Choose a topic, and see if writing in a different place or using different tools makes a difference in your creativity, productivity, or writing. Try writing in three different places.

6. *Take a break:* After you have been writing for a long time, leave the writing alone for twenty-four hours. Come back to it, and start to write again. Then record if the break made a difference.

PLAGIARISM

When you decide to present someone else's ideas as your own without giving the source, it is plagiarism.

- **When you use another's work, word for word, without providing the source, it is plagiarism.**

- **When you copy a report (full or partial) from another student, it is plagiarism.**

- **When you insufficiently paraphrase a paragraph without citing the source, it is plagiarism.**

Plagiarism is morally wrong, and most colleges and universities punish students who plagiarize. Sometimes, however, plagiarism occurs because you are not sure what should be cited and what should not. By following the Modern Language Association of America (MLA) or the American Psychological Association (APA) guidelines you will be less likely to make mistakes.

Before you plagiarize, remember that there is a tremendous pride that comes from creating a work that is totally your own. If you make the decision to plagiarize, you must also take personal responsibility for the punishment that could include failure on that specific project or failure in that class. Some colleges and universities dismiss or suspend students for repeated offenses.

Plagiarism is not only wrong, it does not allow you to create, learn, or advance. By choosing to plagiarize you are preventing yourself from participating in the educational system that you have worked so hard to enter. Professors do not like "cheats" and neither do employers.

PLAGIARISM is presenting someone else's ideas and words as your own, without source citations.

This chapter has presented a variety of techniques that you can use in all of your writing endeavors. You will find that your writing improves as you read, research, outline, create, free-write, edit, rewrite, edit, and write again. Good writing comes from being willing to practice your writing skills until excellence permeates each written product.

Step Inside . . . The Library

The library is a great place to read, conduct research, study, relax, listen to tapes, learn new things, and have fun. Listed here are some of the resources you can find at the library.

On-Line Catalogue

Increasingly, the catalogue of library holdings is available on-line. The catalogue usually lists books, journals, reference materials, CDs, records, tapes, and other formats. The on-line catalogue has taken the place of the card catalogue in many libraries. The on-line catalogue will show you where materials are located and if they are available.

Computerized Databases

Databases are updated weekly or quarterly. They may have newspaper articles covering material on the local, national, and international levels. One educational database—Educational Resources Information Center (ERIC)—consists of abstracts of educational journals that are useful for research in teaching and education.

Other databases could include InfoTrac, Magazine Index, Business Index, corporate and executive profiles, management case studies, or industry analysis. By using a computer, you can access a list of subjects. When you find relevant ones, insert a CD, and the article may be available for your review on the screen. If the library has this information, you can print it out, but be aware that some libraries charge a fee for the printouts. Make sure that the original source is written on the printout so that you can cite it accordingly. If the library does not have the needed article, the staff may be able to order it for you.

Interlibrary Loan

If your library does not have a book that you need, a librarian can order it from another library and usually have it for you quickly. Clarify with the librarian how long it will take, as sometimes it takes days, and other times it takes months. There may be a fee for this service.

Encyclopedias

Encyclopedias offer basic research material that provides you with a foundation to start more specific research.

Next time you need a quiet place to study, do research, or just sit and think, check out your library.

Internet Exercise

Access the Web site for your college. Look up the school's policy on plagiarism, and answer the following questions.

1. What is your college's definition of plagiarism? In your own words provide two examples that would apply to this definition.

_____

_____

_____

_____

_____

_____

_____

_____

2. What is the penalty for plagiarizing?

_____

_____

_____

_____

_____

3. What else does this Web site tell you about plagiarism?

_____

_____

_____

_____

_____

Role Play   Allison

Break into groups of four or five, and read aloud the setting and role play. You will need to create the ending of this role play through discussion and collaboration in your group. You may change the dialogue and add new characters. Your role play conclusion should demonstrate that you have reflected on the character's perspective and her circumstances. Then, act out the role play for the class. When you have finished acting out the role play, answer the questions.

Setting: *Allison and Xi are drinking coffee in the student center.*

Allison is a first-semester college student. In three of her courses, term papers have been assigned. Allison hates writing papers. She had her sister help her with a mandatory English paper her senior year in high school. This semester, one of her term papers has been returned with a large, red D at the top. Allison has two more papers to write.

Xi is in her sophomore year at the same college. Allison knows her from high school. Xi has always received good grades. She wrote for the high school newspaper.

Allison: Thanks for meeting me, Xi.

Xi: Well, anything for a graduate of Everett High. So, how can I help you?

Allison: I am having lots of trouble with my classes. I never knew there would be so much writing involved. I am really good at Scantron tests, but putting a paragraph together is tough.

Xi: You just have to practice writing. The more you write, the easier it becomes.

Allison: I wanted to show you a paper I just got back. [*Hands her the paper*] I got a D. The instructor also wrote the word *plagiarism*. What does that mean?

Xi: Well, *plagiarism* means you have stolen someone's words or ideas.

Allison: I don't get it. How are you supposed to write on a topic you have no knowledge about without using someone else's information?

Xi: That's where citing sources and paraphrasing comes in.

Allison: I don't get it; I had a bibliography at the end.

Continue the dialogue. Xi can clarify source citations and paraphrasing in addition to giving Allison more tips on writing research papers.

Questions

1. When is it important to cite sources?

2. What role do note cards play in the writing of a research paper?

3. How would you answer Allison's question: How are you supposed to write on a topic you have no knowledge about without using someone else's information?

Review

This review is correlated with the objectives at the start of the chapter. One way to study Chapter 7 is to look at the objectives, write down everything you learned about each one, and then compare your notes to this review.

1. *Writing is a way of life.* The letters, reports, research papers, or notes you take are based on your writing skills.

2. *Clarify assignments.* Be sure to clarify assignment expectations before you start to write. At the very least, understand what type of paper has been assigned, what topics are allowed, how many sources you will need, and how long the paper should be.

3. *Follow the writing guidelines* as you complete writing assignments.

4. *Writing steps.* Choose a subject, narrow the subject, create a thesis statement, do the research, take research notes, outline and organize, write a first draft, proofread, seek constructive criticism, revise, and write and hand in a final draft.

5. *Manage your attitude:* Sometimes attitudes interfere with writing. Do not give up! Instead, write, take a break, and write again. As you stick with it, ideas will flow easily. Stay motivated and maintain a positive attitude.

6. *Combat writer's anxiety* through free-writing, free-talking, writing yourself a letter about the topic, reading about the topic, changing writing techniques, and taking a break.

7. *Plagiarism* is presenting someone else's ideas or words as your own without source citations.

CHAPTER 8

Relationships

OBJECTIVES

By the end of this chapter, you will be able to . . .

1. **Understand the importance of relationships in college.**

2. **Identify the characteristics of effective communication.**

3. **Understand the parts that empathy, active listening, selective listening, and paraphrasing play in communication.**

4. **Learn how to resolve conflicts: create win-win situations, display a sense of humor, find mutual goals, separate the people from the problem, seek alternative solutions, and use the six C's of conflict resolution.**

5. **Recognize date rape and learn how to prevent it.**

RELATIONSHIP CHECKLIST

The purpose of the following checklist is to help you understand how to create good relationships.

Check the appropriate answer:

1. Do you maintain eye contact when talking to others? YES _____ NO _____

2. Do you show genuine interest in what others are saying? YES _____ NO _____

3. Do you plot responses while others are still speaking? YES _____ NO _____

4. Do you speak before you think? YES _____ NO _____

5. When you feel frustrated or angry, do you start your sentences with *you*? YES _____ NO _____

6. Do you look at others, act as though you are listening, yet not hear one word? YES _____ NO _____

7. Do you listen only to ideas with which you agree, tuning out ideas with which you disagree? YES _____ NO _____

8. Do you paraphrase others' words in order to understand them better? YES _____ NO _____

9. Do you try to create win-win communications? YES _____ NO _____

10. Do you use humor in appropriate ways to break through conflict? YES _____ NO _____

If you said no to questions 3, 4, 5, 6, and 7, and yes to questions 1, 2, 8, 9, and 10, you have many of the skills needed to participate in positive relationships. Based on the checklist, which behaviors would you like to target to improve your relationships?

_____

_____

_____

_____

_____

An important characteristic of a good student is to
develop relationships in class in order to get more out of
the whole academic experience. It is easy to attend class, take
notes, and then go home. But it is not all that easy to interact
in class and form friendships with classmates.

Carol Lindow, student
MORAINE PARK TECHNICAL INSTITUTE, FOND DU LAC, WISCONSIN

Study and writing strategies, time management, and problem solving are the back-bone of academic goal achievement. Relationships are the muscle supporting that academic backbone. Constructive interactions between yourself and your class-mates, college staff, and instructors are essential to claiming victories in college. In fact, creating positive relationships and maintaining them are an integral part of living. Few goals can be achieved without human interaction, effective communi-cation, and the ability to resolve conflicts.

Relationships in college inevitably provide growth experiences. Whether you are living on your own for the first time or returning to school after years in the corporate world, you will encounter new relationship experiences. Relationship challenges can include

▶ Understanding instructor-student interactions, including the instructor's un-written rules.

▶ Learning to live with roommates who are different from you.

▶ Adjusting to leaving that "special someone" back home.

▶ Struggling to find good-quality family time as well as study time.

▶ Interacting in small groups for assigned projects.

▶ Working as a member of a study group.

▶ Participating in student activities and clubs.

Attending college often alters the nature of old relationships and provides the be-ginning of new ones. Creating positive relationships is an adventure that has both its struggles and its rewards.

Group Interactions

As a student as well as in life you will experience many group interactions. Group interactions test your communication skills and challenge your ability to relate to others. Group dynamics exist in dorms, classroom settings, and social activities. Group activities have many similarities to teamwork projects in companies. Learn-ing to work well in groups is an important lifelong skill.

The point of most groups is to work toward a common goal and have fun to-gether with minimal conflict. Study groups are an example of working together for a common goal. When group members come together with different perceptions and ideas, conflicts often surface within the group. Differing opinions always occur, and an effective group always makes the most of this. For a group to work well, each individual must assume responsibility for his or her own positive communication while using problem-solving strategies to accomplish group goals.

Effective Communication

Good relationships do not just happen. They must be created. The major aspects of creating positive relationships are effective communication and conflict resolution. In *Supervisory Management*, Robert Maidment (1995) states, "At least 75 percent of each workday is consumed by talking and listening. 75 percent of what we hear we hear imprecisely. And 75 percent of what we hear accurately we forget within three weeks. Communication is the skill we need the most at work and is the skill we most lack."

The most important communication strategy is the willingness to work at listening to and understanding what others are saying before responding to their message. It is helpful to put yourself in the place of the person talking. This is called *empathy* and is a valued skill in communication. When you pay attention to the other person's feelings, his words may take on a clearer meaning. If you deny the emotions of the other person, you are devaluing his words, and the conversation can become stilted or defensive (Lussier, 1996).

A professor of management at Virginia Commonwealth University, C. Glen Pearce, suggests that in order to be empathic when communicating with others, you should avoid judgment. Often, the other person just needs someone to listen without values or opinions attached. An empathic listener does not have to agree or disagree with the speaker but does need to express a sense of understanding (Reece and Brandt, 1996).

In college and professional relationships it is important to be communicative and understanding. The problem is knowing where to draw the line. At times, it may feel too risky to empathize or care; it may seem easier and safer to keep to yourself and not show your vulnerable side. However, when you allow yourself to risk and share your own emotions in a trusting, safe relationship, it can be very rewarding. Knowing what is appropriate in relationships is often helped by practicing the following communication strategies.

> **EMPATHY** is the ability to identify with what others are experiencing.

EFFECTIVE COMMUNICATION STRATEGIES

AN EFFECTIVE COMMUNICATOR
- displays consistent eye contact.
- does not interrupt.
- pays attention to the spoken word and its message.
- has an appropriate tone of voice.
- shows interest in what others say.
- does not mentally plot answers as others are speaking.
- listens without passing immediate judgment.
- does not finish the speaker's sentence for him or her.
- enjoys others' conversations.
- communicates understanding through responses such as "I understand," "I get it," and "I see what you mean."
- thinks before speaking.
- matches body language with emotions and words.
- listens with empathy or understanding.

Source: Adapted from Robert Lussier, *Human Relations in Organizations: A Skill-Building Approach,* Third Edition. Copyright © 1996 by Irwin. Adapted from Robert Maidment (1995), "Listening to the Overlooked and Underdeveloped Other Half Talking," *Supervisory Management,* 4:22, 278–295.

You/I Messages

For better communication, start speaking with the word *I* instead of *you.* If you start out with *you,* the other person is put on the defensive, which means he or she feels emotionally attacked. Then, to protect his or her self-esteem, he or she creates words to prove he or she is really a good person and that the other person is at fault. Examples of "you" messages are "You are mean" and "You are stupid." Defensive responses might be "I am not mean, but you certainly are!" or "I got an A in Biology; what's your problem?" Defensive comments often take you back to childhood responses, not adult problem-solving responses.

By starting with *I,* the communication promotes sharing instead of creating defensiveness. Using *I* encourages smoother communication, especially when there is stress, anger, or frustration in the discussion. By stating, "I feel . . . ," "I want . . . ," "I think you are saying . . . ," "When I . . . ," you are taking responsibility for the problem rather than blaming the other person. Sometimes, it helps to state your specific emotions or feelings in an "I" message ("I feel angry," "I am frustrated"). Open the communication further by asking a reflective question. "What do you think?" "How do you feel about this?" "Do you agree?" Reflective questions prompt openness rather than defensiveness. This keeps the person with whom you are communicating open to hearing your words.

Active Listening Versus Selective Listening

Strive to be an active listener. Active listening means literally hearing and understanding what the other person is saying. It is easy to look at someone, nod your head, act as though you are listening, and not hear or understand a word. It takes more energy to be attentive and truly care about the meaning or intent of someone's words. By paying attention and listening, your comprehension of information will increase, and you will be appreciated in relationships because you care enough to listen.

HOW DO YOU CHANGE A "YOU" MESSAGE INTO AN "I" MESSAGE?

"**You** are not listening to me, and **you** do not even look at me when I speak to you. Don't **you** like me anymore?"

Try the following "I" message instead:

"**I** enjoy communicating with you, but **I** feel frustrated that you do not look at me when we talk. It makes me feel that my words are not important. Is there a way to work this out?"

PEANUTS reprinted by permission of United Feature Syndicate, Inc.

Effective communication is the foundation of strong friendships.
© Jean-Claude Lejeune.

Reprinted by permission of Gary Hoskins.

SELECTIVE LISTENING is a communication process in which the listener makes a choice to pay attention only to information that is of interest or agrees with his or her own opinion.

Try to refrain from selective listening. This occurs when you listen only to ideas that agree with your own thoughts or perceptions, tuning out those that disagree. When ideas are presented that are different from your personal beliefs, it is important to continue to listen to the ideas. By trying to understand others' ideas and perceptions, you often learn more about them and yourself.

Paraphrasing

PARAPHRASING is a communication process in which the listener restates the essence of the message heard.

Be open minded when listening to others. This can be difficult to do, especially when anger enters the conversation. One way to stop the Ping-Pong effect of throwing angry words at each other without listening is to paraphrase. Paraphrasing is repeating the words or concepts presented by the speaker. By paraphrasing the words that you hear, you can clarify your understanding of the intended message. Once you clarify the message, you will be ready to respond. This process prevents conflicts and increases goodwill in relationships. For instance, consider these words of an instructor to a student who entered his classroom late:

> I cannot believe you walked into my class late, started talking to people who were already taking the test, and then loudly asked to borrow a pencil. What were you thinking? That is not how one acts in a classroom!

The student could paraphrase in the following way—not defensively—to defuse the situation:

> I'm sorry. I understand that you are upset with me because I disturbed your class with my lateness and my talking.

> Learning to communicate effectively is the first step in working out conflicts in relationships. It is up to you to make choices that will improve your communication with others. By practicing these communication strategies, you will find less frustration in your communication and more fun in your relationships.

Active Listening and Paraphrasing

The purpose of this exercise is to practice active listening and paraphrasing.

Break into pairs and decide who will be the listener and who will be the speaker; then follow these directions:

1. Choose a topic of interest to you and your partner. It should be an issue about which you have strong feelings or that might elicit a debate. Decide who will begin, and then alternate speaking roles.

2. (Paraphrasing) Talk to your partner about your chosen topic for one minute. Do not let the listener interrupt you. Ask your partner to rephrase what you said. Discuss the accuracy of the paraphrasing. What ideas were misinterpreted, totally wrong, or simply skipped?

_____

_____

_____

_____

3. (Active Listening) Choose another topic and speak for one minute. Ask the listener to provide as many specific details as possible from your communication. Have the listener discuss the details from your message.

4. Write about this communication experience. Discuss how paraphrasing and active listening could change communication styles.

_____

_____

_____

_____

_____

Conflict Resolution

Buddha stated, "Hatred is never ended but by love, and a misunderstanding is never ended by an argument, but by tact, diplomacy, conciliation, and a sympathetic desire to see the other person's viewpoint." His words resonate today as the essence of conflict resolution.

No relationship exists without conflict. It is naive to believe that when you love someone you will never disagree. Conflicts often occur when motivations or needs are different or misunderstood. Whether conflicts arise with loved ones, study partners, roommates, or business associates, it is crucial to work out each conflict as a team desiring conciliation. Clearly, understanding the motivation or the cause of the conflict is the beginning of conflict resolution. It is this understanding that creates better relationships at college, home, or work.

Conflicts can shake you up and make you question the strength of a relationship, causing doubts about yourself and others. Conflicts are often related to power and control issues. When a conflict affects your relationship, you may feel a loss of control and a mixture of intermingled emotions. Some common ones are anger, love-hate, envy, greed, or impulses to strike out at the person frustrating you. In creating healthy relationships you need to acknowledge emotions, learn to curtail impulses, and find more adaptive ways to deal with frustrating conflicts through conflict resolution.

Instead of letting anger or impulsiveness rule, strive to figure out solutions that will increase the effectiveness of your relationship. Whether your instructor talks too fast, or your roommates eat the food you just bought, or your wife does not want you to attend school, solutions can be found. Here are some basics for resolving conflicts.

Create Win-Win Situations

Negotiate ways in which both of you can be winners. Saying "Do it my way or no way" fosters anger and distrust. Learning to compromise builds respect, trust, effective communication, and positive attitudes based on mutual solutions (Reece and Brandt, 1999).

EXAMPLE

Conflict: Two students are working on a project for their cultural diversity class. They meet in class and decide that one will conduct a cultural interview and the other one will type the paper. When they reconvene, they find out that they had miscommunicated and both have done the same part of the project. Each conducted an interview, and neither wants to type the paper. Each is angry at the other for misunderstanding the division of the tasks.

Action: They discuss the problem and confront the issue at hand: Who will type the paper? They both admit that they had misunderstood their roles in the project.

Resolution: They decide that each will type his or her own paper on his or her cultural interview. Then they will bring their disks to the university lab and work together to effectively combine both interviews into one.

Display a Sense of Humor

Appropriate use of laughter is a strength in dealing with conflicts. Laughter can break up a tense moment and make conflict easier to deal with. Laughter makes you feel better and can be a stress buster. Your ability to be humorous lessens the emotional load that you carry and can alleviate anger that might be projected on others when you feel irritable. Your positive attitude may even be contagious in helping others look at the lighter side of issues.

EXAMPLE

Conflict: John and his son Robert are both at the University of Illinois. John has gone back to earn a Ph.D. degree in developmental education, and Robert is a freshman majoring in journalism. They share a computer at home, and Robert has inadvertently crashed the system. All of John's assignments and projects were stored on the hard drive and are irretrievable.

Action: Robert tells his father about the crash as soon as he comes home from school. At first, John becomes very angry and starts yelling at Robert. John is also angry at himself because he has not created any backup disks.

Resolution: As John is yelling at Robert, he notices that his son has a sign in his lap and a smirk on his face. The sign says "Do you really think that the kid who loves you would do this on purpose?" After reading the sign, John starts to laugh. The look on Robert's face reminds him of all the times his son has caused mischief and has apologized. Even though John is still irritated, he laughs. The humor in the situation reminds him that nothing can be done, it deescalates his anger, and it puts the situation into perspective. ■

Find Mutual Goals

Relationships can become conflictual and strained when one person cannot accept the other's goals. When you work together on things in which you are both interested, you emphasize the similarities in your relationships rather than the differences. This will often carry over into other areas in your relationships in which there are more differences of opinion. Finding mutual goals and acknowledging your similarities gives relationships the strength to continue in less mutual areas.

EXAMPLE

Conflict: Kelly is working part time and has recently started night college. Her husband, Mike, is glad that she is going back to college, but he is not happy about the consequences for him. Now he must combine his full-time job with picking up the children after school, fixing dinner, and getting the children into bed at night. He feels that she has it "easy." He would love to be able to go back to school and not have to work. Kelly worked full time and took care of the kids while Mike finished his B.A. degree. She feels it is only fair that Mike support her now while she attends college.

Action: After fighting for weeks, they decide to sit down, problem solve, and find an appropriate solution.

Resolution: Mike and Kelly compromised. Mike will support her in school, but when she graduates it will be her turn to support him when he returns to college for his M.A. degree. By doing this, both will be able to achieve their goals. ■

Do Not Blame the People; Attack the Problem

Be harder on the problem than you are on the person. By being empathic and accepting of others' perceptions and emotions, you make the problems easier to understand (Kolb et al., 1995).

EXAMPLE

Conflict: Carrie is angry that her instructor is always ten minutes late to class. She believes that his lateness reflects his lack of professionalism.

Action: Carrie goes to the dean's office to inform the dean of her instructor's constant tardiness. Carrie is told by the dean's secretary that she cannot talk to the dean until she has discussed the issue directly with the instructor. Carrie sees the instructor during his office hours. Carrie tells the instructor that she is concerned about his tardiness and knows that there must be a solution.

Resolution: The instructor informs Carrie that he is always late because his daughter's day care center opens at the same time that the class starts. Immediately, Carrie's anger at the instructor dissipates, and she suggests he tell the class about his time crunch dilemma. The class agrees to start ten minutes later than usual so that the instructor can drop off his daughter and arrive at class on time. ■

THE SIX C's OF CONFLICT RESOLUTION

CONTROL: Control and power are central issues in conflicts. When you feel that another person has more control over your life than you do, you may feel frustrated and angry. You may decide to assert yourself and regain control over your life by losing your temper. This will likely affect your relationship with the other person in a negative way. A more effective method in dealing with the situation—before you lose your temper—is to count to ten, walk away, or sleep on the situation. Do something that will give you a break from the conflict and time to gain a clearer perspective. Take control of conflicts by adapting to the situation, by problem solving, and by adjusting your behavior.

COMMUNICATE: Talk through problems. Do not ignore them and hope they will go away. Pay attention, listen, empathize, care, and think before you respond. Choose your responses with respect for others. It is only through effective communication that conflicts will dissipate.

CREATE: Be creative. Problem solve to work through conflicts. The right answer may not be the easiest one. Brainstorm as a team, taking into consideration everyone's needs, not just yours. Refrain from blaming. Instead, use positive problem-solving techniques.

CHOOSE: Use the words "I choose" as you sort through conflicts. ("I choose to problem solve"; "I choose to become angry"; "I choose to listen.") Change conflicts into choices. Brainstorm in such a way that the choices you finally make bring about positive results for all concerned.

CHANCE IT: Follow your heart and give your solution a try. If it does not work, do not blame each other. Try again and again.

CONSIDER ADVICE: Some relationship conflicts are too large! Ask for help from a professional counselor or therapist. It takes strength to face problems and solve them instead of ignoring them or running away from them. Sometimes, problems cannot be faced alone. Know when it is time to seek help. Often, counselors are available on campus to help you work through conflicts.

Source: Adapted from the Illinois State Police, *Six Steps to Solving a Conflict.* 1995.

Seek Alternative Solutions

By seeking solutions, the focus is shifted away from the problem to a future solution. Another way to look at this is to agree to disagree on the problem, but agree to agree on a potential solution. To do this, do not force your solutions or avoid other solutions. Instead, discuss all solutions openly and see which ones are most effective. Come to an agreement on a solution, and create an action plan to implement it. Make an agreement to change and then follow through on your word. You might feel that it is easier said than done, but you can make changes if the relationship is important enough to you (Lussier, 1996). Do not make a commitment to someone unless you intend to follow your words. Your word represents you.

> **EXAMPLE**
>
> **Conflict:** Miguel takes a test in his sociology class and thinks he has earned a perfect grade. When he gets the test back, he finds that an answer was marked wrong that he knows is right. When the instructor reviews the exam, Miguel points out that the question really has two correct answers. The instructor agrees that there could be two correct answers, but he will accept only the one mentioned in class.
>
> **Action:** Miguel goes to see the instructor during his office hours. He asks for further clarification of the instructor's decision to allow only one correct answer.
>
> **Resolution:** The instructor says that there is nothing he can do about the recent exam conflict. However, he promises that from now on he will check an exam more carefully to make sure that no question has more than one correct answer. Miguel is pleased that the instructor keeps his word, and on future tests the conflict never occurs again. ■

These conflict resolution guidelines can be used in intimate, professional, social, educational, parental, and work relationships. Respect is the key issue in all relationships. One way to show respect is by accepting and adhering to the limits set by others. Understanding each other's expectations, values, morals, and comfort levels are key factors in building and maintaining relationships.

Date Rape Can Be Prevented

DATE RAPE is forced intercourse with a nonconsenting person who is an acquaintance or friend.

If respect is lost, communication becomes confused, value systems become altered, and relationships may falter. One example of this is date rape.

Consider the following case report:

After the Community Organizers Conference at Lakeside College, Fred, a short, ruddy-complexioned, twenty-two-year-old man approached me and asked me to go out with him to a local bar for a drink. Even though I had only met him twice before, I felt that I should go with him; after all, he was the conference chairman. Somehow, it seemed rude to say no. In the back of my nineteen-year-old mind, I thought that going with him could help me weasel my way into speaking at the conference the following year.

Once we got to the bar, he quickly drank two beers. Although I wanted to talk about the conference, his main interests seemed to be hunting and beer, not community organization. After he had downed six beers to my one, I told him that I wanted to go home. As he took his car keys from his pocket, I yanked them from his hand and assertively said, "No way are you driving!" The only reason he gave up the keys was because the bouncer at the door told him to listen to me. He did. He handed me the keys without further protest.

As I drove away from the bar in his blue, beat-up Ford truck, I wondered what would happen next. I decided to drop Fred and his truck off at his house, call a cab, and go straight home. The night, however, did not turn out to be as I had hoped. As we were driving down mountain roads toward his house, he asked me to pull the truck over to look at the view from the mountain top. I did as he requested. As we sat there, he started to make passes at me. I told him no, but he didn't believe that I meant it. He persisted. When I said no again, he forced himself upon me and had sex with me against my will.

(Excerpted from the diary of a college freshman, November 2, 1996)

The behavior of the male and female outlined in this diary excerpt exemplifies how sexual scripts can become dangerously confused.

The following research was cited in Laura Snead's *Date Rape: College's Dirty Secret* (1997):

Mary Koss, a researcher at the University of Arizona, conducted the largest study of date rape on college campuses. Koss surveyed thirty-two campuses for *Ms.* magazine and estimated that one in six college women become victims of rape or attempted rape—that statistic has since increased to one in four. Koss found that most rapes occurred on campus. Eighty-four percent of the women knew their assailants but only 27 percent realized that their sexual assault fell within the legal definition of a crime. . . . One in twelve college men responding to the same survey admitted committing acts that met the legal definition of rape or attempted rape, but only one percent of those men saw their behavior as criminal.

If males refuse to believe that women really mean no when they say no, they are participating in faulty sexual scripts. Men may think that women say no because they are attempting to cover their promiscuity. Men may believe that script and force women into sex that could culminate in date rape.

Not only do sexual scripts play a part in date rape but the incidence of date rape increases when alcohol is involved. Drinking inhibits decision making and alters perceptions in ways that prevent the victim from being aware of what is going on. Under the influence of alcohol, women find it more difficult, if not impossible, to be clear in setting and keeping limits. Also, a woman's partner is less likely to hear what she is saying. However, alcohol use does not diminish personal responsibility for making good decisions.

Date rape can be prevented only by heightening awareness in all dating situations. Women need to be able to say no and mean it. Men need to understand that being turned down for sex is not meant as a blow to their self-esteem.

Sue agreed to have a drink with Fred because she thought it could advance her career. Fred went out with Sue for unknown reasons, but his reasons were undeniably different than Sue's. Sue might have been better off meeting Fred in his office the following week to discuss community organization. This decision would have allowed her to meet her professional goals while maintaining her safety. Date rape can be prevented by making informed, insightful decisions that are communicated effectively to one's partner. If date rape does occur, it needs to be reported.

The confusion that surrounds the label "rape" is what makes date rape difficult to report. The Illinois Coalition Against Sexual Assault (1995) states that less than 2 percent of date rapes are reported to the police. Yet, 21 percent of women raped by strangers report the crime to the police. The victims may feel ashamed and believe that they have inadvertently done something to cause the sexual assault. Sex without mutual consent is against the law. Date rape is punishable by law and by campus policies. The act of reporting a date rape may prevent others from becoming victims.

It was 2 a.m.
She was in my room.
We were drunk.

Tell it to the jury.

Tell them whatever you want, but if you have sex
with a woman without her consent, you could be
· arrested, charged and convicted of rape. And then
you can tell your family and friends goodbye.

Against her will is against the law.

This tagline is used with permission from Pi Kappa Phi.

©1992 Rape Treatment Center, Santa Monica Hospital.

If you have been assaulted, seek counseling to overcome your emotional
trauma and to help you through the healing process. Most college campuses have
services available to help you deal with date rape or sexual assault. Talking about
the pain is important so that you can go on with the rest of your life. You may feel
that you do not want to tell others, or that it is your fault. With counseling, you
can come to terms with rape and its effects on you. Through community rape centers, student services offices, campus health care centers, or community emergency
rooms, you will be able to seek and find the medical and emotional care that you
need. Date rape is too much of a trauma to deny and suppress. The victimizer may
also want (or be ordered by the court) to seek counseling (Worth, 1995).

Through daily interactions we weave the essence of our lives. The ability to feel
genuinely good about our communication with others, the inner contentment
that is felt with the honest resolution of relationship problems, and the concern
and support we receive from others are the factors that provide strength in trou-
bled times, so that, as Oprah Winfrey says, "You can dance when it's all over."

Rape 101.

If you think rape can't happen to you, you're in for a real education.

Because statistics show that a college-aged woman is vulnerable to rape. Very often by someone she knows. A fellow student. Even a date.

And that's a crime. Because any time a woman is forced to have sex against her will it's a felony.

Rape. It's a subject no one should take lightly.

©1995 Rape Treatment Center, Santa Monica, CA

Step Inside . . . Activities and Organizations (Clubs)

Whenever I speak to alumni from the college at which I teach, one of the first things they mention are the relationships that they created while in college. They are quick to mention who they have spoken to recently, and they ask which professors are still teaching, and then they want to know if the clubs to which they belonged still remain on campus. The college experience is learning based, yet the relationships created through clubs are often maintained or remembered with fondness years later.

Even though you are very busy, do not forget to make the time to find out about clubs and organizations on your campus. One way to do this is to visit the clubs on Club Day or ask various people who have joined clubs their opinions of the best ones on campus. If you have never skied, you may want to join the ski club just so you can try it. Give the drama club a chance. Act in a play instead of thinking that one day you might like to act. There are always clubs available in your major (math, computers, French) that are great to join because they will provide you with additional skills. Plus, it looks good on your résumé.

Interview three people from three different clubs, and record the information that you found out about each club. State if you would join this club and the reason for your decision.

_____

_____

_____

_____

_____

_____

_____

_____

_____

_____

_____

_____

_____

_____

_____

_____

_____

_____

_____

_____

_____

_____

_____

_____

_____

_____

_____

_____

Internet Exercise

Choose one of the following topics and find an article on the Internet about it; write a three-paragraph summary of the article (include the author, address, date, and title of the article).

Conflict resolution

Effective communication

Building positive relationships

Date rape

_____

_____

_____

_____

_____

_____

_____

_____

_____

_____

_____

_____

_____

_____

_____

_____

_____

_____

_____

_____

_____

_____

_____

_____

Role Play Suzanne

Break into groups of four or five, and read aloud the setting and role play. You will need to create the ending of this role play through discussion and collaboration in your group. You may change the dialogue and add new characters. Your role play conclusion should demonstrate that you have reflected on the character's perspective and her circumstances. Act out the role play for the class. After each group has acted out its role play, discuss the questions that follow.

Setting: *Suzanne and her mother, Roberta, are talking in Suzanne's room.*

Suzanne, aged nineteen, is an honors student in her second semester at college. She has been awarded an academic scholarship for her sophomore year. Recently, her father became ill and died suddenly.

Roberta is fifty-two years old. The loss of her husband was a great shock to her, and because of the new financial situation, she will have to work full time. She has asked Suzanne to stay at home and care for her four siblings, aged seven, nine, eleven, and thirteen years, while Roberta works.

Suzanne: I was just looking at some of these old photos. I miss Dad so much.

Roberta: So do I. Oh, Sue, I miss him very much.

Suzanne: [*Hugs Roberta*]

Roberta: It is very hard on me. I will have to go to work full time. And I know it will not be easy on you and the other children.

Suzanne: It's funny how you still see me as a child. I like it somehow. It makes me feel secure.

Roberta: I'll always be there for you, Suzanne.

Suzanne: And, I will be there for you, Mom.

Roberta: I know, sweetheart. I need you very much.

Suzanne: You will always have me, Mom.

Roberta: I have to ask you something very important, Sue. I want you to know that I wish I didn't have to ask this of you, but I have no choice.

Suzanne: What is it?

Roberta: Sue, I need you back home to take care of the other children.

Suzanne: I'm here, and I'll be here all summer to help out.

Roberta: Sue, I need you back home, for good.

Suzanne: What do you mean "for good"?

Roberta: I need you to quit school for a while.

Continue the dialogue. Include both Suzanne's perspective and her mother's.

Questions

1. Describe the dilemma in which Suzanne finds herself.

2. How do you feel about her mother's request? How do you think Suzanne feels?

3. What compromise can Suzanne and her mother reach?

Review

This review is correlated with the objectives at the start of the chapter. One way to study Chapter 8 is to look at the objectives, write down everything you learned about each one, and then compare your notes to this review.

1. *Creating constructive, positive relationships* with others is an important part of college and life. Relationships are the muscle supporting the academic backbone.

2. *Effective communication* depends on maintaining consistent eye contact, not interrupting, paying attention to the spoken word and its message, using appropriate voice tone, showing honest interest, listening with empathy and without judgment, enjoying conversation, thinking before speaking, and matching body language with emotions and words.

3. *Active listening* really means hearing and understanding what the other person is saying. *Selective listening* occurs when you listen to ideas that agree only with your own thoughts or perceptions and tuning out those that disagree. *Paraphrasing* is repeating words or concepts presented by the speaker.

4. *Conflict* can be a sharp disagreement or opposition of values, interests, goals, or ideas. *Conflict resolution* is working together to find ways to resolve problems. *Basics for resolving conflicts:* create win-win situations, display a sense of humor, find mutual goals, separate people from the problem, seek alternative solutions, and use the six C's of conflict resolution: control, communicate, create, choose, chance it, consider advice.

5. *Date rape* is forced intercourse with a nonconsenting person who is an acquaintance or friend. Date rape happens more often when one or both persons involved have been drinking alcohol. It can be prevented by heightening awareness in all dating situations.

CHAPTER 9

Staying Healthy

OBJECTIVES

By the end of this chapter, you will be able to . . .

1. Identify the cause of stress.
2. Deal with stress more easily.
3. Recognize emotional conflicts.
4. Know more about caring for your emotional and physical health.
5. Integrate a nutritional plan into your lifestyle.
6. Take care of yourself by exercising often.
7. Know what HIV is and how to prevent it.
8. Comprehend the effects of substance abuse on the human body.

WELL-BEING CHECKLIST

The purpose of the following checklist is to help you analyze your knowledge about healthy lifestyles.

Check the appropriate answer:

1. Do you believe that your mental attitude can affect your physical health? YES _____ NO _____

2. Do you find time daily to do something enjoyable? YES _____ NO _____

3. Do you think your attitude, perceptions, and temperament can increase and decrease stress? YES _____ NO _____

4. Is the "college 15" an honor that students receive after finishing fifteen credits? YES _____ NO _____

5. Is it true that you *cannot* get HIV from coming in contact with sweat, tears, or urine unless they contain blood? YES _____ NO _____

6. Is it true that you *cannot* get HIV from a mosquito bite? YES _____ NO _____

7. Are flu-like symptoms, unexplained tiredness, swollen glands, a dry cough, unexplained weight loss, or unusual spots on the skin or in the mouth symptoms of HIV? YES _____ NO _____

8. Is peer pressure to drink alcohol still prevalent on college campuses today? YES _____ NO _____

9. Do you think it is true that people who have attended college drink more alcohol than those who have not? YES _____ NO _____

10. Do you think it is true that people who have not attended college take more illicit drugs than those who are college educated? YES _____ NO _____

If you answered yes to every question except 4, you have a good understanding of health facts. If you answered no to questions 1, 2, 3, 5, 6, 7, 8, 9, or 10, go through the chapter to find the correct answers and write them here. Then write down the reasons you agree or disagree with the chapter.

_____

_____

_____

Effective students take responsibility for all that happens in
their life. When something goes wrong, they don't lay
blame on others or themselves; instead they seek solutions to
their problems. This includes health consciousness. They take
care of their bodies and nourish them with the proper
amount of fuel and rest needed to survive. They admit their
fears but do not dwell on them. Accepting them and letting
them go gives [these students] more courage to strive, excel,
and continue to grow.

Mary Nanette Alaniz, student
WESTERN WYOMING COMMUNITY COLLEGE, ROCK SPRINGS, WYOMING

The better you feel and the sharper your mind, the easier it is to achieve personal victories. It is difficult to feel victorious in college when you feel physically or mentally depleted. Physical and emotional health are just as important as study strategies in creating college victories. Emotional conflicts, depression, stress, or illness can interfere with the concentration you need to do well.

This chapter explores aspects of mental and physical well-being and their significance in meeting the challenges of life. It also presents stress management suggestions, ways to recognize emotional illness, and information about the prevention of HIV and AIDS.

Emotional Health

A STRESSOR is anything that causes stress.

The emotional side of life is bound to the physical. Health is connected directly to emotions, feelings, stress level, and psychological needs. When you become angry, your face turns red. When you are sad, you cry. When you are stressed, tension headaches develop. These are signs that your body is responding to psychological stressors. Stressors are stress-causing events. Acknowledging and understanding emotions, feelings, and psychological outlooks will help you claim a healthy lifestyle.

Stress Management

EUSTRESS refers to good stress.

STRESS is a force exerted by internal expectations or external pressures that coerces individuals to adjust, adapt, or cope.

Everyone experiences stress differently. When you are stressed, how do you feel? Tense, depressed, irritable, overwhelmed, overly tired, or sleepless? Or does stress feed your motivation, confidence, and desire to finish tasks? College is an experience that can be simultaneously rewarding and stressful. Stress is defined as a force exerted by internal expectations or external pressures that coerces individuals to adjust, adapt, or cope. Stress is not all bad. Sometimes eustress motivates you to study, practice formulas, read, give a speech, or prepare for tests when you would rather be out having fun. Moving to a new home, starting college, changing jobs, divorce, marriage, and pregnancy are big changes that can cause positive and negative stress.

Continuous change and cumulative negative stress correlate to physical illness or emotional distress (Selye, 1976). Fifty to eighty percent of diseases have a stress-related element (Juzwin, 1998). Stress can send messages in the form of pain. If stressors in your life have become too overwhelming, they may manifest within the body as depression, increased daily anxiety, fatigue, irritability, excessive worry, headaches, stomachaches, or sleep problems. By understanding what causes stress while seeking ways to deal with it, you will be able to deflect its negative impact.

What Causes Stress?

QUICK CHECK

List three stressors in your life.

1. _____

_____

2. _____

_____

3. _____

_____

List one thing that you can do to combat each stressor.

1. _____

_____

2. _____

_____

3. _____

_____

The causes of stress differ for everyone. What stresses one person may not stress another. Where one student sits quietly and methodically answers difficult test questions, another skips with increased anxiety from question to question until the pages blur. Why does the first do so well and the second falter? Responses to stress may be related to your personality, attitude, and temperament. Your personality filters thoughts, perceptions, and responses that allow you to control or lose control of stress-filled or anxiety-related situations.

Pressure and stress come from you, not from the events in your life. Events in life do not have the power to stress you out or give you a headache. It is your reaction to stressors that causes emotional or physical pain. Stress is created by choosing to have a stressful or nonstressful response to events. The level of stress in life is greatly influenced by attitude. Use the words "I choose" to help understand this concept. For example, you *choose* to let yourself get frustrated over an instructor whose attitude you do not like; you *choose* to overeat or to buy more CDs at the store than you can afford. It is not the instructor, the food, or the CDs that cause the stress. It is your reaction that increases or decreases stress levels.

Your temperament, your built-in natural way of being, responding, and thinking, has a great deal to do with how much stress your body and mind believe and perceive. For example, a student who has taken notes, attended lectures, and studied extensively may think, "I know I am going to fail this test. When I fail this test, I will feel so incompetent that I will fail the next one, too." The student has prepared for the test. He needs to change his negative thoughts by believing and perceiving that the test can be conquered. It is time for him to sit back, feel confident, and think, "Don't worry; be happy; I will do well." Worrying builds stress and increases anxiety; it does not change stressful situations. If you cannot change the problem, stop worrying. Worrying serves no useful purpose. Creating positive logical solutions, making smart choices, and creating positive attitudes go a long way toward eliminating stress. Beyond personality and perception, stress can be caused by the following.

Lack of Control over Situations.   Feeling you are in a situation that you cannot control (poor grades, too many bills, not being able to find child care, abusive relationships) increases stress levels. The less control you feel, the more stress you will probably confront.

Taking on More Than You Can Handle.   Taking on too many responsibilities (raising a family, going to school full-time, keeping house, and working part-time) raises stress levels, as does feeling that you have too many things to do in too little time. Reevaluate the tasks that you need to complete, and decide if there are some that you can eliminate.

Putting Yourself Last.   By meeting your needs last, your stress level increases. If you take care of everyone else before you take care of yourself, stress will find you.

Perceptions and Expectations Not Matching Reality.   Having expectations of yourself that are incongruous with the realities of your behavior (wanting to get A's in college without studying) is a stress factor.

Being a Couch Potato.   Do you find yourself reading, watching TV, playing video games, or sitting at your computer more than you do walking, stretching, running, or playing active sports? Inactivity may correlate to higher stress levels.

Exhaustion.   Stress increases when you do not get enough sleep. Irritability and frustration increase as required sleep decreases. Pushing yourself to meet deadlines may be a part of life, but there must be a constant evaluation process that monitors your exhaustion and frustration level. There may be times that sleep and health are more important than that omnipresent deadline.

Fear.   Fear breeds stress. It is a simple formula: the more fearful you are, the more stressed you may become. (This is obviously not true for everyone. If it were, why would you want to go to a horror movie?) Fear relates to math and text anxiety; it may also relate to the anxiety associated with trying new things, such as projects, speeches, and labs. Acknowledging and understanding fear is the first step toward becoming victorious when battling stressors in your life.

Withdrawing and Keeping the Pain Inside.   There are times to take a break from stressful events, and there are times to attack them head-on. It is not always a conscious decision; in fact, withdrawal or confronting of stressors may be related directly to the coping mechanisms that you learned when you were young. The struggle comes in deciding when to pull away from painful events to analyze them more thoroughly or when to share painful events with others as you strive to work them out.

Taking Life Too Seriously.   Sometimes the only way to lift pain caused by stressors is to look for a lighter side. It is difficult to look for laughter when everything seems bleak, yet bringing laughter to problems helps you evaluate stressors with a clearer mind.

In 1983, Martin and Lefcourt conducted a study in which they asked college students to fill out self-report scales about their sense of humor. The students also participated in behavioral assessments that measured the ability to exhibit humor in stressful situations. The researchers found that students who could create humor in stressful situations were less affected by negative events than students who could not integrate humor into their stressful lifestyle (Martin and Lefcourt, 1983; Rathus, 1993).

Ways to Deal with Stress

Focus and Take Control.   What can you do to change the stressors in your life? If you cannot change the problems, let go of the frustration. Do not obsess over the negatives. Negative thoughts and constant worry drain the energy you need to study and feel good about yourself. The more upset you let yourself become, the harder it may be to stop the frustration cycle. Refocus, take control of your thoughts, and understand the true priorities in life. When you take control of stressors, you find a fresh perspective that provides the strength to carry on.

QUICK CHECK

List three effective ways to deal with stress.

1. _____

_____

2. _____

_____

3. _____

_____

Why do they relieve stress?

_____

_____

_____

_____

_____

Prioritize Tasks.   If you attend college while working or caring for a family, time organization is a must. Prioritize and evaluate tasks, then make choices. When there are not enough hours in the day, which is more important: playing with the kids or studying for a biology test? They could be equally important. If you choose to play with the kids, enjoy each moment with them; do not feel guilty about not studying because guilt increases stress. The pleasure derived from being with them might provide enough energy and joy to allow you to concentrate on biology later. An important part of prioritization is focusing on what you are doing, enjoying it, and then moving on to the next task. Do not allow the multitude of tasks to stress you so much that none of them get done. By prioritizing the tasks that need to be completed and sticking with the to-do list, you will be more organized and less overwhelmed.

Make Sure You Are Number One on the List.   Relax and enjoy! Take time daily to care for yourself. This might involve sitting by the window and watching the sunset, enjoying hobbies, taking a bubble bath, or rollerblading with a friend. It is important to find time for yourself. No matter how much you need to get done, try to schedule time for relaxation, joy, and fun. As you relax, push the worries of the day out of your mind. Give yourself permission to feel good and have fun. While you are relaxing, do not dwell on the problems or mistakes made during the day. After all, you are human, and you need some quiet guiltless time to reenergize.

Ask yourself daily, "What happened that was good today?" Oprah Winfrey encourages her TV viewers to write down three good things that happen daily. Dr. Andrew Weil (1998), author of *Spontaneous Healing and 8 Weeks to Optimum Health*, states that you should "get your priorities in order, and that means nurturing yourself first." Sometimes the to-do list takes over and life satisfaction and happiness become lost. Continue to work toward your goals daily, but try to make time to appreciate yourself and the good things in life, no matter how big or little. As you look for the good in each day, the bad carries less weight within your heart and life satisfaction increases, good thought by good thought.

Monitor Your Perceptions: Are They Based on Reality?   Be honest with yourself by acknowledging your weaknesses and evaluating the best way to keep them in perspective. If, for example, you tell your advisor that your goal is to achieve an A in math, and you attend class only 40 percent of the time, the expectations may not be real. You may want that A badly, but it will be difficult to achieve if you are not in class. You may believe that you will attend classes, but 7:00 A.M. classes are a stark reality that you do not seem to be able to deal with well. To adjust the reality to your perception, it might be better to schedule later classes next term, because you know yourself well enough to know that no matter how great your intentions are, you probably will not make 7:00 A.M. classes. By honestly evaluating perceptions, understanding yourself, and accepting or challenging limitations, you can change behaviors and consequently reduce stress.

ENDORPHINS are morphinelike chemicals that fight depression and produce pleasure naturally.

Exercise.   When you exercise, endorphins, morphinelike chemicals that fight depression and produce pleasure naturally, are produced in your body. Exercise has a way of making stressors seem less menacing. Try to exercise daily, twenty minutes each time (with a doctor's approval). You might be amazed at how exercise makes you feel better, blows away anxiety, and creates serenity.

Sleep on It.   When things are stressing you out, take a quick nap or go to sleep for the night. The sleep process suspends stress, and you will be able to put the problem in better perspective when you wake up. Sleep provides a natural time-out from the stressors in your life.

Do Not Let Fear Control You.   Stress is stronger and harder to manage when you live in fear. Fear is a natural reaction to any event that seems threatening. Fear can help you stay alert and alive in some situations and cause thinking distortions in others. Put your fears in proper perspective. Fears of not being successful can be turned into behaviors that will make sure that you are successful. Feeling upbeat and positive can deter fears. Sometimes unrealistic expectations and false perceptions are fears' foundation. When you attack the inconsistencies that live within your fears, put reality back into your perception, check your thinking processes, and learn to believe in your choices, fear subsides (even when you make mistakes, because your mistakes become your teachers).

Exercising even ten minutes two or three times a day will fight stress.
© Ariel Skelley/ THE STOCK MARKET.

Share Your Problems with Others.   Talk to others. When you are with people you like, stress seems to melt. Pick out people that are fun to be with and are trustworthy. By sharing your problems with others, the burdens you feel seem to be lifted. You may feel a sense of relief from stressors after sharing and conversing with those who care about you. Their positive energy may be contagious.

Laugh.   Laugh, laugh, and laugh again. Feel better? Laughter provides avenues to purge stressors. Laughing at yourself takes away guilt, anger, frustration, and fear. Laughter allows you to take yourself less seriously while creating new perceptions of stressful situations.

Do Something Nice for Others.   Volunteer to work at the pediatric wing of a hospital, provide transportation for the elderly, tutor children, read to those who cannot, smile to those who will not, give to your favorite charity, work in a soup line. Giving to others decreases your pain and replaces it with a warm heart and a gentle smile.

When you are sharing thoughts with friends, stress seems to vanish.
© José L. Pelaez/THE STOCK MARKET.

EXERCISE

How Do You Deal with Stress?

The purpose of this exercise is to help you identify stressors in your life and find ways to classify, understand, and resolve them.

1. List the most stressful event in your life at present.

_____

_____

_____

_____

_____

2. Why is it stressful?

_____

_____

_____

_____

_____

3. Can you change it? Do you have control over it? Explain.

_____

_____

_____

_____

_____

4. List three ways that you could resolve this stressor. Include factors like change of perception, change of behavior, or change of goals. What is one step that you can start today to change this stressor?

_____

_____

_____

_____

_____

_____

_____

_____

Recognizing Emotional Conflicts

No one wakes up in the morning and chooses to have emotional conflicts that interfere with daily functioning. However, many people have disorders that cause them to be depressed, disoriented, and sometimes delusional.

There are many misconceptions about the recognition and treatment of emotional disorders. As a result, you may fail to take note of important symptoms among friends, relatives, or yourself, thus delaying treatment.

The following list of symptoms related to emotional conflicts may help you identify those you know who could be suffering from dysfunction in their lives. The sooner you can identify the problems, the sooner you can help them find treatment.

▶ Loss of appetite

▶ Sleep problems

▶ Deep mood swings

▶ Extreme energy or lack of energy

▶ Feelings of consistent sadness

▶ Constant fear

▶ Feelings of anxiety for no reason

▶ Repetition of strange obsessive rituals

▶ Frequent panic attacks

▶ Hearing voices, imagining things that are not really there

▶ Delusions that someone will attack soon (Davis and Palladino, 1994)

If you or someone you care about is experiencing these symptoms on an extended basis (fear is common; experiencing fear so intensely that you cannot leave your house for days is an extended problem), it is important to find support as you work through problems. In *Psychology* (Davis and Palladino, 1994), psychotherapy is defined as "a special relationship between a distressed person and a trained therapist in which the therapist aids the client in developing awareness and changing his or her thinking, feeling and behavior." Finding a therapist, going into therapy, and getting help may be important to emotional health, especially if constant depression,

PSYCHOTHERAPY is a process in which a clinical therapist provides support and guidance for those experiencing anxiety or emotional problems.

▶ *Fruits.* Recommended: two to four servings daily. Examples of servings are 1 piece of fruit or a melon wedge, ¾ cup of juice, ½ cup of canned fruit, ¼ cup of dried fruit.

▶ *Breads, Cereals, Rice, Pasta.* Recommended: six to eleven servings daily. Examples of servings are 1 slice of bread, ½ cup of cooked rice or pasta, ½ cup of cooked cereal, 1 ounce of ready-to-eat cereal.

The portions that you eat may be more than one serving. For example, when you supersize your order at a fast-food restaurant, you know that the servings are much larger than usual. Each of the food groups provide some, but not all, of your needed nutrients; that is why it is important to eat from all of the food groups daily. Be aware that nutritional needs change if you are very active, pregnant, or elderly.

By eliminating some of the fat in your diet and eating more of the healthy foods, you will feel better. If you mix good nutrition with exercise, you will find the results to be even more significant.

HOW MUCH FAT IS IN THAT FOOD?

INSERT THE AMOUNT OF FAT GRAMS YOU THINK EACH OF THE FOLLOWING FOODS CONTAINS.

1. 1/2 cup potato salad _____ grams
2. 1 cup whole milk _____ grams
3. 2 oz. processed cheese _____ grams
4. 1 egg _____ grams
5. 1/3 cup of nuts _____ grams
6. 1 tsp. jelly _____ grams
7. 1/4 whole avocado _____ grams
8. 10 French fries _____ grams
9. 2-crust fruit pie (1/6 of an 8 in. pie) _____ grams
10. 2 oz. doughnut _____ grams

Please see page 179 for the answers.
Source: Adapted from D. Powell, J. Karwan, and S. Ryskamp, "Eating Plans," *The HealthyLife Weigh.* © 1994. American Institute for Preventive Medicine.

BURNING CALORIES

HOW LONG WOULD A 130-POUND WOMAN HAVE TO DO THE FOLLOWING EXERCISE TO BURN OFF 100 CALORIES?

1. Walking upstairs at one step per second _____ minutes
2. Weeding a garden _____ minutes
3. Watching television _____ minutes
4. Vacuuming _____ minutes
5. Walking at 3 mph _____ minutes

Please see page 179 for the answers.
Source: Adapted from D. Powell, J. Karwan, and S. Ryskamp, "Eating Plans," *The HealthyLife Weigh.* © 1994. American Institute for Preventive Medicine.

inner conflicts, insurmountable fears, drug abuse, violence, or inability to monitor anger interfere with you or a loved one's ability to function on a daily basis.

The Consumer's Guide to Psychotherapy (Engler and Goleman, 1992) recommends three things to think about when deciding to enter therapy:

1. Is your level of distress intense enough that you want to do something about it now?

2. Are you no longer able to handle your problems on your own? Do you feel the need for more support?

3. Is your distress affecting your personal life, family, or work?

If the answer is yes to any of these questions, you may want to seek a therapist. One of the best ways to find a good therapist is to ask friends, family, or your doctor for recommendations. Your campus may have a counseling center, or your Student Services Office may be able to make a referral for you. Most therapy sessions are short-term, and therapists help clients work through problems by assisting in creating solutions that will make life more agreeable.

EXERCISE

Emotional Health

The purpose of this exercise is to clarify your understanding of emotional health.

Create a role play similar to the ones at the end of each chapter. Use the theme "emotional health" to create the background, characters, and setting. Then create the dialogue. At the end, write about what you learned from doing this exercise.

_____
_____
_____
_____
_____
_____
_____
_____
_____
_____
_____
_____
_____
_____
_____
_____
_____

Physical Health

Success in college ties into the decisions that you make about your own physical and mental well-being. Your energy level, your ability to pay attention, your motivation, and your ability to work hard depend on your physical and mental health. Your body is the vehicle that carries you toward your goals, and if you do not take care of it, your goals may become elusive. Eat right, sleep as much as you need, take time to exercise, and learn about factors that affect your physical health. This is all part of a healthy lifestyle.

Nutrition

Eating in a healthy way gives you the energy you need to study and do well. (Remember, Mom used to tell you that, too!) Have your friends ever said, "What can I do about the Freshman 15?" They are referring to the pounds that students seem to gain when they are away from home for the first time, or when they start eating their own cooking or dorm food. Eating out or snacking on high-fat or calorie-laden foods often puts pounds on and may not provide you with the kind of nutrients your body needs. For example, a Double Whopper with cheese contains 890 calories and 55 grams of fat; one medium slice of thin-crust pepperoni pizza contains 230 calories and 11 fat grams (Powell et al., 1994). It is difficult to always eat correctly, but you will find that you feel better and have more energy when you do. Try to resist the temptation to skip breakfast; your body needs the fuel to get you through the day. Remember, the way you feel correlates with the way you perform.

Food Guide Pyramid.   The Food Guide Pyramid was developed by the United States Department of Agriculture and the Human Nutrition Information Service. It includes daily recommended servings from six basic food categories:

▶ *Fats, Oils, Sweets.* The small tip of the pyramid uses symbols to illustrate fats, oils, and sugars. Examples of these are cream, butter, margarine, soft drinks, and candies. Alcoholic beverages are also part of this group. These foods are calorie laden and contain few nutrients, so their intake should be limited. Some fat or sugar symbols are shown in other food group sections. That is to remind you that some foods in those groups can also be high in fat and added sugars. For example, sugars are found in cheese, juices, or ice cream, and fats are found in French fries, whole milk, or hamburgers. When you choose foods, remember that the fat and added sugars should be chosen from all of the food groups, not just those at the top of the pyramid.

▶ *Milk, Yogurt, Cheese.* Recommended: two to three servings daily. Examples of servings are 1 cup of yogurt or milk and 1½ to 2½ ounces of cheese.

▶ *Meat, Poultry, Fish, Dry Beans, Eggs, Nuts.* Recommended: two to three servings daily. Examples of servings are 2½ to 3 ounces of cooked lean meat, poultry, or fish. A ½ cup of cooked beans, 1 egg, or 2 tablespoons of peanut butter is equivalent to 1 ounce of lean meat.

▶ *Vegetables.* Recommended: three to five servings daily. Examples of servings are ½ cup of chopped raw or cooked vegetables and 1 cup of leafy raw vegetables.

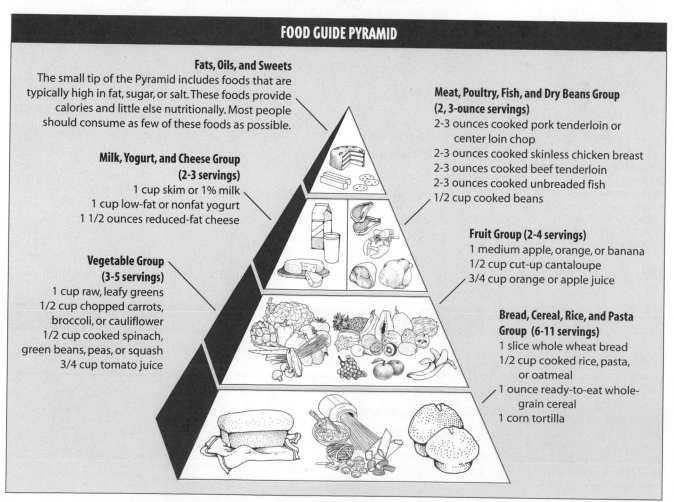

Source: Adapted from the U.S. Department of Agriculture, *The Food Guide Pyramid.*

Nutrition

The purpose of this exercise is to monitor your nutritional intake.

Pick a forty-eight-hour period and record *all* of the foods that you eat. Be sure to read labels or ask for nutritional contents in restaurants so that you can record calories and fat grams.

	First Day List all foods and drinks you had today. Record fat grams and calories for each.	**Second Day** List all foods and drinks you had today. Record fat grams and calories for each.
Breakfast		
Lunch		
Dinner		
Snacks		
Miscellaneous		

Compare your list with the Food Guide Pyramid. What will you need to change in your diet to create a healthier menu? Of which foods did you have too few? Too many?

_____

_____

_____

_____

ALTERNATIVE EXERCISE

IN ADDITION TO YOUR REGULAR EXERCISE ROUTINE, TRY SOME OF THESE:

- Take the stairs instead of the elevator.
- Set the timer and see how fast you can clean your apartment or house. (Quickly washing windows, scrubbing floors, or vacuuming burns calories.)
- Walk briskly around the building during class breaks instead of going to the student union to get a candy bar.
- If you drive to school, park your car far from the building.
- Ride a stationary bicycle while watching TV.
- Go to the mall to walk, not shop. Do not let window shopping slow you down.
- Invite friends to your home or dorm room, to dance!
- Play a sport or go skating or swimming instead of watching a movie.

Exercise

Exercise is an important part of a healthy lifestyle. Exercise benefits you not only by relieving stress but also by increasing your flexibility, cardiovascular fitness, weight control, and muscle strength. The fitness activity you choose (racquetball, aerobics class, step class, walking, jogging, basketball) is up to you. Knowing that the more you exercise, the healthier you will be should keep you motivated to take the extra time to exercise. The benefits of exercise are so great that you need to find time to include exercise in your schedule. When you exercise, you not only feel better but you also look better and become more energized.

If you are one who likes to sit and vegetate, it is time for you to acknowledge the importance of exercise and begin to integrate it into your life daily. Start the first day with ten minutes of exercise and then build up to twenty minutes or more a day. You will notice the difference; you owe it to yourself to make the commitment and take the time to take care of yourself. As you take care of yourself, your studying, test taking, and stress management become easier to control.

In Green and Winfrey's book *Making the Connection: Ten Steps to a Better Body and a Better Life* (1996), the very first step is to exercise aerobically five to seven days each week. When you exercise in the morning, you get your metabolism going for the whole day.

Some common excuses for not exercising are, "I hate exercise," "I do not have the time," "It is boring," "I would rather read a book." Do you exercise as often as you can, or do you create excuses, too? Whenever you know you should exercise but look for excuses not to, create exercise goals: write down the reasons that exercise should be a part of your daily routine and paste them on your mirror as a daily reminder. Include exercise in your daily planner so you do not forget. Create time to exercise with coworkers (instead of eating lunch) or as a family-oriented activity (rollerblading, bicycling, or family football games). Remember it takes only twenty to thirty minutes of exercise a day to feel better, be more energized, and stay mentally focused.

AIDS and HIV

When you take responsibility for your lifestyle, you must not only exercise, learn effective measures to fight stress, and eat nutritiously, you must also be knowledgeable about AIDS. According to *Time* magazine, "AIDS is now the leading cause of death among Americans aged 25 to 44, surpassing accidents" ("While AIDS Takes Its Toll," 1996).

AIDS (Acquired Immunodeficiency Syndrome) is a disease that causes the body to lose its natural protection against infection. A person with AIDS is more likely to become ill from infections and unusual types of pneumonia or cancer that healthy people can normally fight off. AIDS is caused by a virus called HIV (Human Immunodeficiency Virus).

What Should You Know about AIDS and HIV?   The American Social Health Association (1991) gives the following summary:

► AIDS is caused by the HIV virus, which attacks certain white blood cells that are meant to protect the body against illness.

► HIV is hard to get. However, both men and women can become infected with HIV and can give the virus to someone else.

► HIV is found in the blood, semen, and vaginal secretions of infected people.

► AIDS is a sexually transmitted disease.

► HIV cannot live on its own or in the air or water.

► You cannot get HIV from being near someone who has it.

► AIDS cannot be ignored; it causes death.

► In the next few years, 90 percent of new HIV infections will occur through unprotected sexual intercourse—heterosexual, bisexual, and homosexual.

► AIDS can be prevented (DuPage County Health Department, 1996).

You *Will Not* Get HIV . . .   (DuPage County Health Department, 1996)

► From clothes, a telephone, doorknobs, a drinking fountain, or a toilet seat.

► From shaking hands, hugging, or being in a crowded elevator with a person who is infected with the virus.

► From coming in contact with sweat, tears, urine, or excrement, unless those substances contain blood.

► From food that has been handled, prepared, or served by a person who is infected with the virus.

► Through everyday contact with people around school, the workplace, parties, stores, or swimming pools.

► Through casual contact with someone infected with HIV.

► From mosquito bites or other insect bites. The AIDS virus is not transmitted through a mosquito's salivary glands like other diseases such as malaria or yellow fever.

► From kissing someone on the cheek. Scientists cannot absolutely rule out the possibility of transmission during prolonged, deep kissing. HIV occasionally can be found in saliva, but in very low concentrations. The possibility exists that cuts or sores in the mouth may provide direct access for HIV to enter the bloodstream during kissing. Still, there has never been a single case documented in which HIV was transmitted by kissing.

You *Can* Get HIV . . .   (Illinois Public Health Department, 1996c)

► From unprotected sexual intercourse (vaginal and anal) with someone who has been infected with HIV.

► From sharing needles during intravenous drug use with someone who has been infected with HIV.

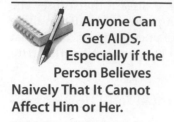

Anyone Can Get AIDS, Especially if the Person Believes Naively That It Cannot Affect Him or Her.

▶ From oral sex with a person who has been infected with the virus. The act often involves semen and vaginal secretions or fluids that contain HIV. During oral sex, the virus might be able to enter the bloodstream through cuts or sores in the mouth.

▶ From birth by an HIV-infected mother. The virus can be transmitted to the baby from the mother before or during birth. It can also be transmitted to the baby through breast-feeding.

General Information about AIDS.   Some people have become infected with HIV from receiving blood. This occurred generally prior to 1986, before blood collection centers began testing donors for HIV.

Some people worry that they may get HIV during dental work. Five patients apparently were infected with HIV while receiving dental care from a Florida dentist who did not use proper infection control techniques. However, the risk appears to be extremely low, since no other cases have been documented during more than ten years of the epidemic.

By the end of 1998, the Joint United Nations Programme on HIV/AIDS and the World Health Organization reported that the estimated number of people living with HIV has grown to 33.4 million worldwide (10 percent more than in 1997). Women represent 43 percent of all people over 15 living with HIV and AIDS. Since the start of the epidemic approximately 20 years ago, HIV has taken the lives of nearly 14 million adults and children. An estimated 2.5 million deaths happened in 1998, more than ever reported in a single year. Health officials predict that everyone will eventually know someone who is infected with HIV ("Common Sense about AIDS," 1992).

How Long Does It Take to Develop the Signs of AIDS?   Persons with HIV can develop signs of infection at any time from months to years after being infected. About half of the people with HIV develop AIDS within ten years, but the time between infection with HIV and the onset of AIDS can vary greatly ("Common Sense about AIDS," 1992).

How Can You Tell If Someone Has HIV?   You cannot really tell if someone has HIV. A person infected with HIV may have no symptoms but can spread the disease. Many people with HIV do not show any sign of infection, but HIV is in their body for the rest of their lives and they can infect others if they engage in behaviors that transmit HIV.

What Are the Physical Symptoms of HIV?   Even if you are infected with HIV, you may feel perfectly healthy, but you could also experience

▶ Flulike symptoms.

▶ Unexplained tiredness.

▶ Swollen glands or lymph nodes.

▶ Continuing fever, chills, or heavy night sweats.

▶ Continuing dry cough or shortness of breath.

▶ Unexplained weight loss.

▶ Unusual spots on the skin or in the mouth.

▶ Continuous diarrhea.

These symptoms could relate to other illnesses. However, if the symptoms persist, it is time to consult your physician (Illinois Public Health Department, 1996c).

What Is an HIV Antibody Test?   The HIV antibody test is a blood test that can determine whether the antibodies to HIV are present in a person's blood. Antibodies are produced after infection with HIV. There is no test for AIDS itself.

You should seriously consider taking an HIV antibody test, if you

▶ Have shared needles or syringes to inject drugs.

▶ Have had sexual relationships with several partners.

▶ Are a man who has sex with other men.

▶ Are a hemophiliac who received clotting factor prior to 1986.

▶ Have had sex with someone who falls into any of the preceding categories.

The decision to take or not to take an HIV antibody test is a personal choice. That is why public health departments around the nation offer testing procedures anonymously. Every person meets individually with trained counselors at various stages of testing before, during, and after the actual blood test (Illinois Public Health Department, 1996a).

How Can You Prevent HIV?   The only sure way to prevent the spread of HIV is not to have sexual intercourse or to have sex only with someone who is not infected and who has sex only with you. At present, the male latex condom is considered the best protection against sexually transmitted diseases. Using latex condoms properly every time you have vaginal, anal, or oral sex, though not completely safe, can greatly lower your risk of infection. When a man cannot or will not use a latex condom, the female condom is the next best choice. Whatever type of condom you use, the most important factor is to use it from start to finish every time you have sex.

Sharing needles or syringes to inject drugs or steroids, even once, can transmit HIV. HIV from an infected person can remain in a needle or syringe and then be injected directly into the bloodstream of the person who uses it next (American Social Health Association, 1991).

What Treatments Are Available?   At present, there is no cure for AIDS; once you have HIV, you are infected for life. However, there is more hope today for treatment than there has been in the past. Dr. David Ho, of the Aaron Diamond AIDS Research Center in New York City, has combined different antiviral drugs into a potent cocktail composed of protease inhibitor, AZT, and another powerful drug called 3TC. Although not everyone responds to this cocktail (some cannot physically tolerate these powerful drugs), the therapy seems to force the disease into remission. If you have AIDS and your body cannot tolerate the new drugs, there are other treatments and medicines that can help your body resist the virus. They do this by slowing the growth of HIV and delaying or preventing certain life-threatening conditions (Illinois Public Health Department, 1996b).

Who Dies from AIDS?   People who have died of AIDS in the United States have been male and female, heterosexual, homosexual, rich, poor, and of all races. AIDS knows no boundaries when it chooses its victims. If you engage in high-risk behavior, you can become infected with AIDS. The male homosexual population was the first in the United States to be affected by the disease. No matter what you have read or what you hear, you must be aware that the number of heterosexual AIDS cases is currently growing (DuPage County Health Department, 1996).

Substance Abuse

Drugs.   Why do you think there were more drug users among individuals aged 16–25 in 1997? Why do you think drug abuse increased significantly among 18–25 year olds from 1979 to the early 1990s? In 1997, an estimated 13.9 million Americans had used an illicit drug one month prior to the interview conducted by the National Household Survey on Drug Abuse, associated with the U.S. Department of Health and Human Services and the World Health Organization. There continues to be concern about substance abuse on college campuses.

SUBSTANCE ABUSE refers to patterns of use that result in negative health consequences.

SUBSTANCE DEPENDENCE involves compulsive use, craving, and increased tolerance.

Substance abuse refers to patterns of use that result in negative health consequences or impairment in social, psychological, and occupational functioning, often resulting in problems in living. Substance dependence involves compulsive use, craving, and increased tolerance. A person who is substance dependent may try to cut back on the drug but not be able to, and may need to continue taking the drug in increasing amounts.

Drugs and alcohol are used as a way to relieve stress or emotional pain. They are also used to feel accepted in social groups or for curiosity's sake ("I just wanted to see what it would do"). The problem is that (1) the pain and stress will still be there to haunt you when you come down from your "high"; (2) being part of that particular group may not be worth the potential side effects and risk of addiction;

SUBSTANCE ABUSE			
	First Time Use	**What Is It?**	**What Does It Do?**
MARIJUANA	Approximately 2.5 million Americans used marijuana for the first time in 1996.	Marijuana is produced from the *Cannabis sativa* plant and is a mild hallucinogenic.	It impairs coordination, perceptual functions, and memory. It causes feelings of anxiety and raises blood pressure.
HEROIN	There were an estimated 171,000 new heroin users in 1996.	Heroin is derived from opium. It is a narcotic analgesic.	It creates a euphoric state. It induces sleep. When consumed in extreme amounts it induces coma.
COCAINE	There were an estimated 672,000 new cocaine and crack cocaine users in 1996.	Cocaine is a stimulant derived from coca leaves.	It creates feelings of euphoria, reduces hunger, falsely increases self-confidence, increases blood pressure, and constricts blood vessels, which decreases the oxygen supply to the heart.
HALLUCINOGENS	There were approximately 1.1 million new hallucinogen users in 1996—approximately twice the average annual number during the 1980s.	Hallucinogens are LSD ("acid"), mescaline, or phencyclidine (PCP). They are plant derived or synthetic.	Hallucinogens produce vibrant, distinct hallucinations. High doses impair coordination and judgment; they alter moods. Those who use hallucinogens can lose contact with reality and experience paranoid delusions.

Do you know what effect drugs can have on the human body?
Source: Adapted from *Grolier Encyclopedia of Knowledge.* Copyright © 1995 by the Grolier Educational Corporation. Adapted from the 1997 National Household Survey on Drug Abuse. Substance Abuse and Mental Health Services Administration. U.S. Department of Health and Human Services.

and (3) "try it and see" is very dangerous: people have become addicted and have even died as a result of experimentation (Worth, 1995).

The most used and abused substance is alcohol, and more than half of all college students choose to use it. Drinking is common on college campuses, even though teachers and parents have been warning students against it since grade school. There seems to be much confusion about alcohol use and what constitutes social drinking versus abuse. In the following list, "one drink" is equivalent to 12 ounces of beer, 4 ounces of wine, or 1¼ ounces of liquor.

▶ *Current use* refers to at least one drink in the past month.

▶ *Binge use* refers to five or more drinks on the same occasion at least once in the past month.

▶ *Heavy use* is defined as five or more drinks on the same occasion on at least five different days in the past month.

In 1997, approximately 111 million people aged twelve years and over were current alcohol users, which, at the time, was 51 percent of the U.S. population. Approximately 31.9 million Americans engaged in binge drinking, and 11.2 million Americans were heavy drinkers. Young adults were the most likely to binge or drink heavily (Substance Abuse and Mental Health Services Administration, 1997).

How do you know if you are an alcohol abuser? You have been abusing alcohol if you are

▶ Experiencing hangovers.

▶ Passing out.

▶ Having alcohol-induced blackout periods of amnesia.

▶ Experiencing an increased tolerance to alcohol (need to drink more to obtain the same effect).

Peer pressure to drink alcohol on college campuses continues to be a source of conflict. As a freshman you might want to investigate the drinking policies and penalties on campus so that you can be aware. Also be aware that when you drink alcohol, your judgment can be affected. One bad decision made while intoxicated can cause you years of repercussions (Worth, 1995).

Alcohol is a contributor to cirrhosis of the liver. Among college students, heavy—that is, binge—drinking may be associated with impulsive behavior, depression or anxiety, drinking in groups, greater sexual aggression, and participation in unsafe sex (Shalala, 1995).

CHUGGING CAN KILL.

Whatever your goals are, try, on a daily basis, to find ways to take care of your-self so that your goals can become real. Goals are easier to achieve when you are feeling well. This can be done by preventing stress, having a nutritious, balanced diet; exercising; taking care of your health; and not abusing drugs.

Step Inside . . . Student Health Services

The Student Health Services system takes the place of your family doctor. When you are away from home and cannot see your own doctor, visit Student Health Services. Whether you need a physical or a vaccine, have a rash of unknown origin, or need a new prescription, this service can meet your needs. It provides free or low-cost HIV screening tests and gynecological services, including birth control pre-scriptions. It is staffed with doctors and nurses, some closely connected with the counseling centers.

Student Health Services is interested in preventing disease and keeping you healthy. Therefore, it offers free seminars on stress management, nutrition, heart disease prevention, weight management, and smoking cessation. Many Student Health Services centers offer aerobics or fitness classes.

Often, colleges are concerned about you during finals and will offer services to support your study effort. For example, some colleges provide fifteen-minute massages to students prior to their final exams to encourage relaxation during tests. Others offer apples or oranges as a healthy snack between finals as alterna-tives to high-fat, high-sugar, high-calorie foods (Elmhurst College, personal com-munication, 1996).

Student Health Services usually offers its services at a reasonable rate or on a sliding scale (based on salary). You might want to contact the health center on your campus before you need it in an emergency to see when it is open and what serv-ices it offers.

Internet Exercise

Using the Web, do the following:

1. Find a Web site that lists ways to stay healthy. List five of its suggestions. List the Web site address and the author of the article.

_____

_____

_____

_____

2. Access a Web site that discusses alcoholism and drug abuse. List a phone number, address, or Web site address that you could contact if you needed help in stopping substance abuse.

_____

_____

_____

_____

Role Play Chuck

Break into groups of four or five, and read aloud the setting and role play. You will need to create the ending of this role play through discussion and collaboration in your group. You may change the dialogue and add new characters. Your role play conclusion should demonstrate that you have reflected on the character's perspective and his circumstances. Act out the role play for the class. After each group has acted out its role play, discuss the questions that follow.

Setting: _Chuck and Anita are in a restaurant._

Chuck is twenty-two years old. He graduated as valedictorian of his high school class. He is now in his second semester at the local university. Chuck earned decent grades his first semester. However, he is barely passing two of his courses the second semester. Lately, he has been partying hard on the weekends with some of his college friends. Chuck drinks heavily at the parties and sometimes passes out. He has now taken to going out during the week. Chuck blames the drinking on the pressures from school and from his father, who wants him to get straight A's.

Anita is Chuck's girlfriend. They first met in biology class last semester. Anita is majoring in nursing. She and Chuck have not been able to see each other for a few weeks because she works the night shift at the local hospital. The last two dates with Chuck were not good. Chuck spent most of the time complaining and drinking.

Anita: I really miss seeing you.

Chuck: The same here. It's hard. Either you're working or I'm studying for some test.

Anita: How did you do on your last test?

Chuck: What? Huh? Not too good. In fact, I failed it.

Anita: That's the third test you failed, Chuck.

Chuck: Don't get on my case, all right?

Anita: No, it's not all right.

Chuck: I need another drink.

Anita: That's the problem. You drink too much.

Chuck: What do you mean I drink too much? I only drink when I want to relax.

Anita: That's not true. You drink when you want to escape or are pressured.

Chuck: Don't practice your Psych. 101 on me, Anita.

Anita: That's not fair. I care about you, Chuck.

Chuck: Good. Can we just drop the whole thing?

Anita: I am not going to drop it. Last time we were together you asked me to look into Alcoholics Anonymous. So I did. There is a meeting next Monday night. If you want, I will go with . . .

Chuck: [*Interrupts*] Since when do you run my life?

Anita: I don't want to run your life, Chuck. I'm just trying to be a friend.

Chuck: I'm sorry, Anita. I'm just not myself.

Anita: What do you think it will take to be yourself again? I can't go on with the person you've become.

   Continue the dialogue. You need not reach a resolution to the problem.

Questions

1. How do you think Chuck has dealt with stress in the past?

2. What do you think Anita's role should be in dealing with Chuck's alcohol abuse?

3. Describe the issues that Chuck is refusing to confront.

4. How should a friend help a person who abuses drugs?

Review

This review is correlated with the objectives at the start of the chapter. One way to study Chapter 9 is to look at the objectives, write down everything you learned about each one, and then compare your notes to this review.

1. *Stress.* Emotional health and physiological health are bound together. *Stressors* are stress-causing events that can cause individuals to act tense, irritable, or tired. Continuous change and cumulative negative stress correlate with physical illness or emotional distress. Stress can manifest itself in the form of depression, increased daily anxiety, headaches, stomachaches, or sleep problems. *Causes of stress:* Pressure and stress come from you, not from the events in your life. Stress is caused by choosing to be stressed or not stressed in response to events. Your temperament—the way you respond and think in the presence of stressors— relates directly to how you perceive stress. Worry builds stress and increases anxiety; it does not change stressful situations. Stress can also be caused by lack of control over situations, taking on more than you can handle, meeting your needs last, being a couch potato, being tired, being fearful constantly, taking life too seriously, withdrawing, and keeping the pain inside for long periods of time.

2. *Ways to deal with stress.* Prioritize tasks, relax and enjoy life, make sure you are number one on the list, monitor your perceptions, exercise, sleep on it, do not let fear control you, tell others about your problems, and laugh and then laugh some more.

3. *Recognize emotional conflicts.* People who are experiencing emotional conflicts may lose their appetite or experience sleep problems, deep mood swings, constant fear, depression, feelings of anxiety for no reason, and frequent panic attacks. They imagine things that are not there, or have delusions.

4. *Psychotherapy* is defined as a special relationship between a distressed person and a trained therapist in which the therapist aids the client in developing awareness and changing his or her thinking, feelings, and behavior.

5. *Integrate a nutritional plan into your lifestyle.* Nutrition is an important part of staying healthy. Stay away from high-fat, high-calorie foods, and try to eat breakfast because it provides you with the fuel that you need for the day. Try to integrate the food groups in the food pyramid into your daily diet.

6. *Exercise* is a benefit because it relieves stress, increases your flexibility, improves your cardiovascular fitness, and increases muscle strength. When you exercise, you will feel better and become more energized.

7. *AIDS* is the leading cause of death among Americans aged twenty-five to forty-four years. AIDS is a disease that causes the body to lose its natural protection against infection. It is caused by the HIV virus, which attacks certain white blood cells that are meant to protect the body against illness. You can contract AIDS from unprotected sexual intercourse, sharing needles during intravenous drug use, or having oral sex with someone who has been infected. HIV may be transmitted to babies from infected mothers before or during birth, or through breast-feeding. Physical symptoms of AIDS are flulike symptoms, unexplained tiredness, swollen glands, continuing fever, chills, dry cough or shortness of breath, unexplained weight loss, continuous diarrhea, and unusual spots on the skin or mouth.

8. *Substance abuse* refers to patterns of use that result in negative health consequences or impairment in social, psychological, and occupational functioning, often resulting in problems in living. Substance dependence involves compulsive use, craving, and increased tolerance. Individuals turn to drug abuse to escape pain in their lives, increase their confidence, give in to social pressure, break boredom, or satisfy curiosity. They may become substance dependent because of addictive properties in the substance, family and peer influences, genetics, or existing psychiatric disorders. Alcohol is the most used and abused substance; more than half of all college students choose to use it. Alcohol is a contributor to cirrhosis of the liver, cancer, antisocial personality disorder, heart damage, and bulimia.

Source: Adapted from D. Powell, J. Karwan, and S. Ryskamp, "Eating Plans," *The HealthyLife Weigh.* © 1994. American Institute for Preventive Medicine.

Answers to "How Much Fat Is in That Food?" 1. (8 grams), **2.** (8 grams), **3.** (18 grams), **4.** (5 grams), **5.** (22 grams), **6.** (0 grams), **7.** (9 grams), **8.** (8 grams), **9.** (19 grams), and **10.** (11 grams)

Answers to "Burning Calories" 1. (14 minutes), **2.** (19 minutes), **3.** (77 minutes), **4.** (17 minutes), and **5.** (27 minutes)

Glossary

Acronym   Word formed from the first letters of key words to encourage memory retrieval.

Acrostic   Sentence or phrase built from the first letters of key words.

Action Plan   Outline of steps that will support the achievement of goals.

Active Listening   Process during which the listener pays attention and mentally registers all verbal and nonverbal communications.

Analyze   To separate into parts and explain.

Association   Connection of a concept you are trying to learn with a memory that is already established.

Auditory Learner   One who learns best by hearing.

Coding   Changing information to make it more memorable.

Cognition   Thinking process like reasoning, knowing, or perceiving.

Compare   To evaluate so that you can find similarities and differences.

Conflict   Disagreement, for instance, between values, interests, goals, or ideas.

Conflict Resolution   Finding ways to resolve disagreements.

Contrast   To find differences between two or more things that are compared.

Cramming   Forcing too much information into a tired brain in a short amount of time.

Critical Thinking   Process in which questioning, challenging, dissecting, and problem solving are important tools for active learning.

Date Rape   Forced intercourse with a nonconsenting person who is an acquaintance or friend.

Defensive   Feeling emotionally attacked; wanting to defend yourself from anguish by using words that will prevent more pain from occurring.

Define   To describe exactly; to state the characteristics or meaning.

Discuss   To provide opinions on a course of action or an issue.

Effective Communication   Process by which information is exchanged. It depends on maintaining consistent eye contact, attending to the spoken word and its message, using appropriate voice tone, showing honest interest, allowing no interruptions, and listening without judgment.

Empathy   Ability to identify with what others are experiencing.

Endorphins   Morphinelike chemicals that fight depression and produce pleasure, naturally.

Enumerate   To name one by one in a specific list.

Eustress   Stress that is good or positive.

Evaluate   To find the value or worth.

Explain   To provide meaning or interpretation. To state reasons for better understanding.

Extrinsic Motivator   External factor that prompts you to strive for goals.

Feedback   Information from others that encourages understanding.

Interpret   To make meaning clear with new or different words.

Intrinsic Motivator   Internal factor that prompts you to strive for goals.

Kinesthetic Learner   One who learns best through action.

Learning Disability   Intellectual handicap that interferes with learning.

Learning Style   Personal method that enhances the ability to learn.

Left-Brain Dominance   Quality of those who are logical, serious, knowledgeable, linear in thinking, structured, organized, and rational.

List   Series of words, names, or numbers, often presented in order.

Long-Term Goal   Task you would like to accomplish in the years to come.

Mnemonics   (ne-MON-iks) Simple associations, rhymes, or aids used to prompt remembering.

Note-Taking   Writing down what you want to remember in a format you can follow later.

Outline   Systematic listing of major and minor ideas or concepts.

Paraphrasing   Process of communication in which a listener restates the essence of the message heard.

Plagiarism   Presenting someone else's ideas and words as your own without source citations.

Prioritization   Combining tasks and time together in an orderly fashion.

Problem Solving   Process that includes finding creative, effective answers to questions, problems, or conflicts.

Procrastination   Delaying completion of tasks.

Psychotherapy   Process in which a clinical therapist provides support and guidance for those experiencing anxiety or emotional problems.

Reiterate   To repeat, rephrase, or restate for the purpose of clarification.

Researching   Finding materials pertaining to your thesis statement.

Right-Brain Dominance   Quality of those who are intuitive; have little sense of time; enjoy music, clutter, and creative thinking; make decisions based on hunches and emotions; and use holistic thinking.

Rote Memory   Mechanical memorization.

Selective Listening   Process in which a listener pays attention only to information that is of interest or agrees with his or her own opinion.

Short-Term Goal   Task you would like to accomplish today, in the next few weeks or months, or during the next year.

Stress   Force exerted by internal expectations or external pressures that coerces individuals to adjust, adapt, or cope.

Stressor   Stimulus that causes stress.

Substance Abuse   Patterns of drug or alcohol use that result in negative health consequences.

Substance Dependence   Compulsive drug or alcohol use, craving, and increased tolerance.

Summarize   To state concisely a main idea, avoiding too many specific details.

Telegraphic Note   Brief written memorandum with no unnecessary words.

Thesis Statement   Brief, one or two sentence, statement describing the topic of a writing assignment.

Time Barrier   Factor that prevents you from finishing tasks.

Time Management Chart   Listing of tasks to be accomplished in a specific period of time.

Visual Learner   One who learns best by seeing (reading, watching, or visually imagining).

Visualization   Creating a detailed picture in your mind; for instance, seeing yourself achieve a goal.

Writer's Anxiety   A physical, fearful reaction to any attempt to write.

References

American Social Health Association. (1991). *HIV/AIDS: Questions–answers*. Research Triangle Park, NC: Author.

Atkinson, R., & Longman, D. (1990). *Reading enhancement and development*. New York: West Publications.

Beatrice, J. (1993). *Learning to study through critical thinking*. Chicago: Irwin Career Education Division.

Broadus, J. (1870). *On the preparation and delivery of sermons*. Excerpted from Collins, W., & Jolliffe, D. (Eds.). (1995). *Rhetoric: Concepts, definitions, boundaries*. Boston: Allyn and Bacon.

Browne, N., and Keeley, S. (1994). *Asking the right questions: A guide to critical thinking*. Upper-Saddle River, NJ: Prentice Hall.

Chaffee, J. (1995). *The thinker's guide to college success*. Boston: Houghton Mifflin Company.

The Chicago Manual of Style (14th ed.). (1993). Chicago: University of Chicago Press.

Common sense about AIDS. (1992, June). American Health Consultants. Supplement to *AIDS Alert*.

Curran, T., & Keele, S. W. (1993). Attentional and nonattentional forms of sequence learning. *Journal of Experimental Psychology: Learning, Memory and Cognition, 19*, 189–202.

Davis, S. (1997). *How to overcome procrastination*. Dissertation, University of Illinois.

Davis, S., & Palladino, J. (1994). *Psychology*. Old Tappan, NJ: Prentice Hall.

DuPage County Health Department. (1996). *How you won't get AIDS*. DuPage County, Wheaton, IL: Author.

Ellis, D. (1997). *Becoming a master student* (8th ed.). Boston: Houghton Mifflin Company.

Engler, J., & Goleman, D. (1992). *The consumer's guide to psychotherapy*. New York: Simon and Schuster.

Ferret, S. (1997). *Peak performance: Success in college and beyond* (2nd ed.). Chicago: Irwin.

Flood, K. (1998, September 21). Surviving college: A parent–student guide to the common pitfalls of life in the dorms. *The Press, Sec. 2*, p. 1.

Friedman, H. S., & Booth-Kewley, S. (1987). Personality Type A behavior and coronary heart disease: The role of emotional expression. *Journal of Personality and Social Psychology, 53*, 783–792.

Gardner, J. (1997). *Your college experience* (3rd ed.). Belmont, CA: Wadsworth Publishing Company.

Gibaldi, J. (Ed.). (1995). *MLA handbook for writers of research papers*. New York: Modern Language Association of America.

Gorman, C. (1996, February 12). Battling the AIDS virus. *Time, 147, 7*, 62–65.

Green, B., & Winfrey, O. (1996). *Making the connection: Ten steps to a better body and a better life*. New York: Hyperion.

Grolier Encyclopedia of Knowledge. (1995). Danbury, CT: Grolier Educational Corporation.

Hunter, I. (1957). *Memory: Facts and fallacies*. Baltimore: Penguin.

Illinois Coalition Against Sexual Assault. (1995). *Acquaintance rape: When the rapist is someone you know*. Funded by the Illinois Criminal Justice Information Authority. Springfield, IL.

Illinois Public Health Department. (1996a). *AIDS antibody testing*. DuPage County, Wheaton, IL: Author.

———. (1996b). *AIDS facts for life*. DuPage County, Wheaton, IL: Author.

———. (1996c). *Is somebody giving you something you don't want?* DuPage County, Wheaton, IL: Author.

Illinois State Police. (1995). *Six steps to solving a conflict*. Springfield, IL: Author.

Israel, P. (1998). *Edison: A life of invention*. New York: John Wiley and Sons.

Jenkins, J. G., & Dallenbach, K. M. (1924). Obviscence during sleeping and waking. *American Journal of Psychology, 35*, 605–612.

Juzwin, C. (1998, December). *Managing holiday stress*. Presentation sponsored by Glen Oaks Hospital, Glendale Heights, IL.

Kolb, D., Osland, J., & Rubin, I. (1995). *Organizational behavior: An experiential approach*. Old Tappan, N.J.: Prentice Hall.

Lareson, M. E. (1973, February). Humbling cases for career counselors. *Phi Delta Kappa, Vol. LIV, No. 6*, p. 374.

Lussier, R. (1996). *Human relations in organizations: A skill-building approach* (3rd ed.). Chicago: Irwin.

Maidment, R. (1995). "Listening to the overlooked and underdeveloped other half talking." *Supervisory Management, 4:22*, 23–36.

Martin, R. A., & Lefcourt, H. M. (1983). Sense of humor as a moderator of the relation between stressors and mood. *Journal of Personality and Social Psychology, 45*, 1313–1324.

Matte, N. L., & Henderson, S. H. G. (1995). *Success, your style! Right- and left-brain techniques for learning*. Belmont, CA: Wadsworth Publishing Company.

Nelson, A. (1998, Spring). Juggling the costs of living away from home. *For the Class of '99 Futures, 1*, 237–253.

Nolting, P. (1991). *Winning at math*. Bradenton, FL: Academic Success Press.

Off the wire. (1995, March/April). *Positively Aware, 8*, p. 5.

1000 more questions and answers. (1989). London: Viscount Books and Hamlyn Publishing Group Limited.

Pauk, W. (1994). *How to study in college* (5th ed.). Boston: Houghton Mifflin Company.

———. (1997). Understanding how we forget. In *How to study in college* (6th ed.). Boston: Houghton Mifflin Company.

Powell, D., Karwan, J., & Ryskamp, S. (1994). Eating plans. *The healthylife weigh*. Farmington Hills, MI: American Institute for Preventive Medicine.

Publication manual of the American Psychological Association (3rd ed.). (1983). Washington, DC: American Psychological Association.

Rathus, S. (1993). *Psychology* (5th ed.). Fort Worth, TX: Harcourt Brace.

Reece, B., & Brandt, R. (1996). *Effective human relations in organizations*. Boston: Houghton Mifflin Company.

———. (1999). *Effective human relations in organizations*. Boston: Houghton Mifflin Company.

Rinehart guide to grammar and usage (3rd ed.). (1993). New York: Holt, Rinehart and Winston, Inc.

Robinson, F. (1970). *Effective study* (4th ed.). New York: Harper and Row.

Selye, H. (1976). *The stress of life* (Rev. ed.). New York: McGraw Hill.

Shalala, D. (1995, July). A message from the Secretary of Health and Human Services. *Alcohol Alert* [On-line] *29*. Available: *http://www.niaaa.hih.gov*. (National Institute on Alcohol Abuse and Alcoholism).

Shepherd, J. (1998). *College study skills* (6th ed.). Boston: Houghton Mifflin Company.

Sinclair, B. (1998, May). Teaching students to be critical thinkers on the Web. *Teaching Professor, Vol. 10, No. 2*, p. 3.

Snead, L. (1997, April). Date rape: College's dirty secret [5 pages]. Available: *http://www.urich.edu/~journal/magazine/4-97/features/articles/f-daterape.html*. (University of Richmond).

Substance Abuse and Mental Health Services Administration. (1997). *National household survey on drug abuse*. Rockville, MD: U.S. Department of Health and Human Services.

Trefil, J. (1992). *1001 things everyone should know about science*. New York: Doubleday.

Trimmer, J. F. (1998). *A guide to MLA documentation* (5th ed.). Boston: Houghton Mifflin Company.

Weil, A. (1998). *Spontaneous healing and 8 weeks to optimum health*. New York: Fawcett Book Group.

While AIDS takes its toll. (1996, February 12). *Time, 147, 7*, p. 63.

Worth, J. (1995). "A matter of substance, using alcohol." *New Student Chronicle*, Washington and Lee University, Lexington, VA, p. 15.

Index